# IMAGES
## of America
# MARINE CORPS
# AIR STATION
# MIRAMAR

2006

**MAJ. GEN. STEPHAN WATTS KEARNY.** Maj. Gen. Kearny's long and distinguished career peaked when he was appointed temporary governor of California after the Mexican-American War in 1846. His career began during the War of 1812 and progressed through much of America's expansion westward. He married General Clarke's (of Louis and Clark) stepdaughter and subsequently explored the Yellowstone and Oregon Trails. Eventually he was appointed as commander of the "Army of the West." Major General Kearny's local historical connection occurred at the Battle of San Pasqual near Escondido, California. One of Kearny's junior officers prematurely attacked a group of fleeing Californios who took advantage of the tactical error and killed 21 of Kearny's soldiers. Capt. Archibald Gillespie, USMC, joined General Kearny at the Battle of San Pasqual, receiving credit for his precision artillery fire that drove off the Californios. This single event provides the Marine Corps' earliest significant connection to the Miramar area and to Kearny. Camp Kearny at Miramar was named in Major General Kearny's honor in 1917.

**COVER:** The flight of TBM Avengers (torpedo-bombers) from VMSB-232 is pictured during World War II. Visible on the tail of these planes is a small white diamond with a red devil.

IMAGES
*of America*

# MARINE CORPS
# AIR STATION
# MIRAMAR

Thomas O' Hara

Published by Arcadia Publishing
Charleston SC, Chicago IL, Portsmouth NH, San Francisco CA

Printed in Great Britain

Library of Congress Catalog Card Number: 2005929345

For all general information contact Arcadia Publishing at:
Telephone 843-853-2070
Fax 843-853-0044
E-mail sales@arcadiapublishing.com
For customer service and orders:
Toll-Free 1-888-313-2665

Visit us on the internet at http://www.arcadiapublishing.com

To the nation's role model—the U.S. Marine Corps.

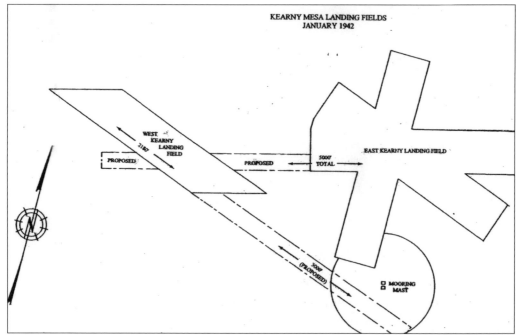

EARLY CAMP KEARNY RUNWAY. Dated January 1942, this early diagram of the Camp Kearny runways and mooring mast provides a glimpse of Camp Kearny's humble beginnings. As the base grew and larger aircraft arrived, the runways and facilities grew to meet the increased requirements.

# CONTENTS

# ACKNOWLEDGMENTS

Thanks go to George "Jorge" Dietsch for his assistance and professional photographic advice. Some data used in this book was obtained from official Web sites. Some images were taken from the U.S. Navy imaging service Web site. Every attempt has been made to credit appropriately.

This book is intended to provide a glimpse of Marine Corps Air Station Miramar, but it is not all-inclusive. In 128 pages, the author has attempted to capture as many highlights as possible, with some of the photographs representing the types of training and events common to Miramar. The author apologizes in advance for whatever has been excluded or overlooked and for any mistakes.

LIFELINE TO THE PACIFIC. Early in World War II, MAG-15 and MAG-25 were created at Camp Kearny to train transport pilot crews and support operations in the Pacific. During the early months of the war, desperate shortages of all sorts were replenished by the DC-3s and C-46 transport aircraft, often by parachute drops. When Marines established a beachhead on Guadalcanal, transport aircraft rushed supplies into Henderson Field and evacuated the wounded. The famous South Pacific Combat Air Transport Command (SCAT) was formed to consolidate air transport efforts in the south Pacific. In the first 18 months, SCAT flew nearly 250,000 passengers and tons of cargo, establishing performance records while supporting Marines fighting the island-hopping campaign. Marine Transport Squadron VMJ-253 established a world record for the longest nonstop, mass flight of 12 R4D Transport aircraft in August 1942 from North Island, California, to Ewa, Hawaii, in 15.8 hours. Typically, fighter aircraft and pilots receive the majority of notoriety during a war; however, the courageous efforts of transport aircrews should not be overlooked.

# INTRODUCTION

In 1911, aviation pioneer Glenn Curtiss was given a three-year lease to use North Island, California, as a base for his aircraft development experiments and pilot training. He set up camp on the south end of the island near the Spanish Bight waterway to work on his seaplanes and build a flying school. Shortly thereafter, Lt. T. G. Ellyson, the first Navy pilot, arrived to begin pilot training and was followed by three Army pilots, beginning the first military aviation school.

In 1912, the Army relocated its original flight school from College Park, Maryland, to North Island and set up an aviation school renting aircraft and hangar space from Curtiss. The Navy sent three more pilots and three aircraft to North Island in 1912, continuing to develop a naval pilot training program. In 1913, the Curtiss lease expired and Glenn Curtiss relocated to Buffalo, New York, but the Army and Navy remained.

In 1912, 1st Lt. A. A. Cunningham, USMC, reported to flight school at Annapolis, Maryland, and Marine aviation was born. In 1916, Cunningham attended the Army Flight School at North Island. The United States entered World War I in 1917, and the emphasis for most military spending, in preparations and support naturally occurred on the Eastern Seaboard, delaying development of West Coast bases. At the beginning of World War I, the Marine Corps had only 5 pilots and 30 enlisted men as aviation assets. By the end of the war, the Corps had 282 officers and 2,180 enlisted men serving in aviation units. Postwar cutbacks decimated all branches of the military, delaying the Corps's eventual arrival on the West Coast with aviation units.

In 1921, a Marine Corps aviation unit was dispatched to Guam to build an airfield, seaplane base, and supporting facilities contributing not only to a forward military presence in the Pacific, but also to the development of the Trans-Pacific aviation industry. In 1923, Maj. Roy Geiger, later to become the commanding general of the 1st MAW on Guadalcanal, led a flight of three Martin bombers across the United States, from San Diego to Quantico, on an odyssey that took 11 days. The flight's arrival in Washington, D.C., received "ceremonial" attention from the crowds, and then the flight continued to their final destination at Quantico. In 1923, the first nonstop transcontinental flight from New York to San Diego occurred, and in 1924 Army pilots departing from Seattle won a race between six nations to be the first to fly around the world, stopping in San Diego on one of their last legs. The race took 175 days, and only the Americans finished.

In 1924, Marine aviation finally established itself on the West Coast when Observation Squadron I arrived on North Island. Additional squadrons were added, and in 1925 the Marine 2d Aviation Group was formed, consisting of an observation squadron, a fighting squadron, and a headquarters squadron. In 1926, the 2d Aviation Group was redesignated as aircraft squadrons of West Coast Expeditionary Forces. North Island Marine squadrons began training in dive-bombing techniques and soon began performing demonstrations up and down the West Coast at air shows and airfield grand openings. In February 1927, Observation Squadron 1 (VO-1M) departed San Diego for Corinto, Nicaragua, during the outbreak of civil war and remained there until June. In April 1927, Fighting Squadron 3 (VF-3M) sailed from San Diego to Shanghai as Marines were deployed from San Diego to China when civil war in that country broke out. Additional aircraft and men from San Diego Marine units augmented the Chinese detachment during the 18-month deployment near Tientsin, China.

During 1927, Ryan Air, makers of the *Spirit of St. Louis*, used Camp Kearny as a testing ground for their prototype aircraft. In May 1927, Charles Lindbergh used Camp Kearny while testing the *Spirit of St. Louis*. In 1928, the Mack Brothers operated a private airfield on the site, and in 1929 the San Diego Air Services Corporation temporarily operated the area, calling it AIRTECH Airport.

In October 1932, the city of San Diego was celebrating Navy Day with the usual fanfare when a flight of 14 Navy aircraft flew over the city and became trapped above the clouds. The spectators watched in horror as the thick San Diego fog rolled in, covering North Island and Lindbergh fields. A local radio station broadcast a Mayday for local automobile owners to proceed to Camp Kearny and surround the field with their headlights shining bright. Thousands of people descended upon the camp, where several of the stranded aircraft landed safely. Shortly after the incident, an auxiliary weather station was established at Camp Kearny to provide pilots with Camp Kearny weather and alternate landing possibilities.

During the early 1930s, the Great Depression knocked the nation to its knees, and appropriations for the military sank to the "survival" level. Many aviation units were decommissioned or absorbed by other divisions. In 1931, Marine detachments from squadrons located at North Island began training aboard Navy aircraft carriers. Marines were deployed on the USS *Saratoga* and USS *Lexington* for the next three years to improve pilot syllabus training and discipline. Air races continued to be very popular during the 1930s and Marines participated whenever possible, winning several trophies.

In 1932, the blimp mooring mast at North Island was moved to Camp Kearny for a visit by one of the Navy's largest blimps, the USS *Akron*, where 25,000 spectators viewed its arrival. Unfortunately, the *Akron* later crashed in the Atlantic. The USS *Macon*, based at Moffet Field, California, used the Camp Kearny mooring mast four times until it crashed off Point Sur, California, in February 1935.

In 1933, the Fleet Marine Force (FMF) was created and replaced the former East and West Coast Expeditionary Forces. The air squadrons of the FMF would be designated as Aircraft One, located at Quantico and Aircraft Two at San Diego.

In 1937, the Marines at Quantico flew all their aircraft cross-country, joining the Marines at North Island, mustering 83 aircraft between them for Fleet Landing Exercise No. 4, held between January 27 and March 10, 1937, on San Clemente Island about 60 miles off the California coast.

In 1939, a final redesignation changed Aircraft One on the East Coast to the 1st Marine Aircraft Group and Aircraft Two at San Diego became the 2nd Marine Aircraft Group. In anticipation of war with Japan in 1940, the Navy began a major expansion at Camp Kearny that was completed only three weeks after the attack on Pearl Harbor.

# One

# EARLY DAYS OF CAMP KEARNY

In 1917, the U.S. Army arrived at Miramar and named the area Camp Kearny, after Maj. Gen. S. W. Kearny. The Army purchased the land for about $4.5 million and then spent $1.25 million developing the staging and training areas at the camp. Over 65,000 men used the facilities on their way to Europe and World War 1. The Army's 40th Division, under Maj. Gen. Frederick Strong and the 16th Division, were Camp Kearny's primary tenants, using the site to train soldiers in infantry maneuvers, tactics, small arms training, and artillery training among a variety of other military subjects and skills. In July 1918, the 40th Division departed Camp Kearny to join the war in Europe. After World War 1, Camp Kearny was used as a demobilization center, and over 16,000 returning servicemen were processed back into civilian life at the camp. By 1920, the nearly 1,200 buildings were torn down and sold for scrap and the Army abandoned the camp. The Army never built an airstrip at Camp Kearny, but aircraft used the expansive parade grounds for landings, practice "touch and gos," and occasionally emergency landings. After the war, the mesa became known as Kearny Mesa, but was used infrequently by the military other than as an outlying practice airfield until the early 1930s, when the Navy began developing their very large rigid-blimp program. In 1934, the Marines established Camp Holcomb on the Camp Kearny site, expanding its training facilities in the area. In 1936, the Navy built the first hard-surface runways on the site. In 1939 with war in the Pacific looming, the Navy purchased additional land to expand the site.

**CAMP KEARNY.** Army Forts, towns, and roads across America are named after Maj. Gen. Stephan Watts Kearny. In 1917, the U.S. Army purchased the mesa in the area named Miramar by Edward Scripps in 1890, and built a military base to train soldiers for World War I. They named the base Camp Kearny. Although they spent $1.25 million, the Army built few permanent buildings operating in simulated combat conditions from tents. The 145th Field Artillery camp is pictured here.

**TENT CAMPS.** Here is another view of the Camp Kearny tent camp and Army personnel loosely marching. Camps like this are still used in the early 21st century for forward combat bases, but modern tents are equipped with heating and air conditioning and can protect inhabitants from biological and chemical weapons.

**PERMANENT STRUCTURES.** Few permanent structures were built when Camp Kearny was constructed, and at the end of World War I those structures were torn down and salvaged by the government. Permanent buildings included the infirmary, the gas station, the post office, the carrier pigeon depot, the theater, and some storage units.

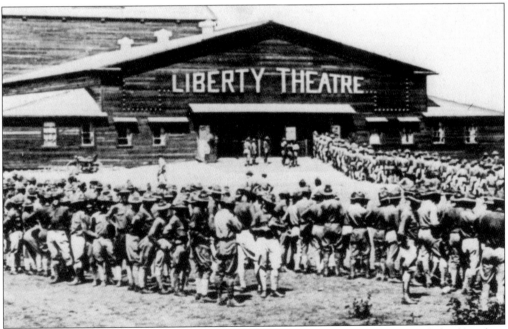

**THE LIBERTY THEATRE.** Silent movies were the craze during World War I, and the long line waiting to enter the Liberty Theatre indicates a box-office hit is playing. Infantry and artillerymen enjoy few amenities throughout training and especially after arriving in the combat zone. The opportunity to view a movie helps morale enormously and relieves some of the daily stress.

**AIR MAIL—CARRIER PIGEON DEPOT.** The carrier pigeon is the long-lost predecessor to the Internet. The carrier pigeon eventually lost its job to the telegraph, the telephone, the radio, and the satellite telephone. But on the battlefields of World War I, the carrier pigeon was most reliable.

**SAVAGE SERVICE STATION.** During World War I, early automobiles and trucks competed with horses and mules for reliability and dominance. At the end of the day, most veterans would take a good mule or a horse over an unreliable horseless carriage and bad roads any day. In this photograph, a Camp Kearny ambulance stops by the service station for a quick pit stop.

**MESS TIME.** Feeding large numbers of soldiers two or three times a day is a difficult task, as with this "field mess," or outdoor dining facility, at Camp Kearny. Add to that task the shortage of running water, fuel supplies, clean preparation facilities, clean washing facilities for those preparing the food, dust, dirt, rain and bugs, and the result is often diarrhea.

**MESS KITS.** Each grunt (soldier or Marine serving in the field) is issued a mess kit. The kit is much like those Boy Scouts use to go camping. While forced marching from place to place or battlefield to battlefield, grunts have been known to lighten their loads and will throw away coats, sleeping bags, ammunition, and even weapons—but no one ever throws away his mess kit.

CHOW TIME. A favorite drink in the military is called bug juice, because at many field dining facilities, the open, 25-gallon vat containing the colored, liquid substance provided for drinking had a thin layer of dead bugs floating on the surface.

GAS WARFARE. Gas-mask training takes place in the Camp Kearny trenches. Soldiers train with gas masks to prepare for the trench warfare encountered upon arriving on the battlefields of Europe. Although total casualties from poison gas were comparatively small, the negative effect on morale was high.

FINAL INSPECTION. These soldiers stand at "present arms" as the colors march past. Notice the early steel helmets that replaced soft covers worn at the beginning of the war. A French officer initially invented the "steel pots" during World War I to reduce casualties from "air bursts" (explosions above ground level) sustained while charging enemy lines.

CAISSONS ON PARADE. A full parade of horse-drawn caissons marches past a crowd sitting in bleachers. The event undoubtedly marked the end of a training period and celebrated the unit's departure to "over there."

**FIRST PLANE TO LAND AT CAMP KEARNY.** In 1918, the first aircraft landed at Camp Kearny. Large crowds gathered, and for many it was the first time they saw a plane at close range. The Army never built an airfield at Camp Kearny, preferring North Island and its proximity to luxurious San Diego to Camp Kearny's hot and dusty mesa.

**SAN DIEGO PARADE.** Camp Kearny soldiers parade through downtown San Diego. When World War I ended in 1918, the Army abandoned Camp Kearny. Over the next 20 years, the site saw sparse use, but when Marine aviation landed on the West Coast at North Island in 1924, the seeds of a brighter future were planted.

# Two

# ROARING TWENTIES AND DEPRESSED THIRTIES

World War I ended with a great victory for the Allies, and tremendous advances in aviation technology were often achieved in blood. However, the lack of vision, political expediency, and the usual cry for a postwar "peace dividend" cut budgets for all branches of the military following World War I. The Roaring Twenties were followed by the Great Depression in the 1930s, and Marine aviation found itself in a survival situation. In 1935, the Marine Corps consisted of only 110 pilots and 1,021 enlisted men. One of the primary reasons for the survival of Marine Air during the 1920s and 1930s was the exceptional vision and intense perseverance of a few great men and a mission. Early Marine aviators like Lt. Col. A. A. Cunningham, Lt. Col. T. C. Turner, and Maj. Roy Geiger held Marine Air together while not only fighting an unsympathetic Congress, but voices within the Corps that didn't appreciate the value of Marine Air. As officer in charge, Cunningham reorganized Marine Air, defined its mission as supporting Marines on the ground, and found one backing up the 1st Provisional Brigade in Haiti, the Dominican Republic, and later Nicaragua, which kept the outfit flying. After battling with Congress for 18 months, the Marine Corps was established at one-fifth the strength of the Navy, with an additional 1,020 Marines designated for aviation. Shortly thereafter, funds were approved for Marine Air stations at Quantico, Virginia, Parris Island, South Carolina, and San Diego, California. In 1924, Marine aviation established itself on the West Coast when Observation Squadron I relocated from the Dominican Republic to North Island, California.

EARLY AVIATION. This picture sets the stage for aviation during the 1920s. The early years, especially post–World War I military aviation, are difficult to comprehend. Even with severe financial cutbacks by Congress there were enormous advances, achievements, and heroics. Air races, air shows, demonstrations, and even the first race around the world took place while civilian pilots wing-walked and barn-stormed their way across the country.

MARINES ARRIVE AT NORTH ISLAND. In 1924, the initial Marine squadron arrived at North Island. Observation Squadron I was the first of the Marine squadrons to take up residence on the West Coast. In 1925, the Marine 2d Aviation Group was formed at North Island, consisting of three squadrons. In 1926, the group was renamed Aircraft Squadrons, West Coast Expeditionary Forces. This photograph shows North Island in the 1930s.

**OBSERVATION SQUADRON I AT NORTH ISLAND.** Close observation reveals the Ace of Spades logo on the tails of these aircraft from Observation Squadron I. This photograph, taken in 1934, shows Observation Squadron I, later designated VO-8M, with two rows of Vought 03U-6 observation aircraft and two Curtis R4C-1 Condors. Observation Squadron I would undergo several name and designation changes over the decades, and eventually became VMA-231 flying Harriers in the 3d Marine Aircraft Wing.

**OBSERVATION SQUADRON I.** Observation Squadron I officers pose at NAS North Island in 1926. The large North Island hangar is in the background.

**OBSERVATION SQUADRON I.** This 1930s photograph shows squadron pilots ready for a mission. The plotting boards carried by each pilot are used to navigate using dead reckoning (DR) navigation techniques. DR navigation amounts to plotting courses and timing air and ground speeds while searching for identifiable landmarks.

**OC2 CURTISS.** This aircraft has the Ace of Spades logo and the markings of VO-8M, as well as a data plate indicating the squadron and station (NAS San Diego). In the upper right corner of the data box is another box containing a triangle, which is a symbol of excellence earned on the gunnery range.

CRASH CREW. A couple of Navy Crash Crew fighters wait "at the ready" for a call. The life of crash crew matches that description of an aviator's life as "98 percent pure boredom interrupted occasionally by 2 percent stark terror." Very often, when the aviator is experiencing the stark terror, the crash crew fighter is trying to save the aviator's life.

UTILITY SQUADRON. Members of Utility Squadron VJ-7M gathered for this 1930s photograph at North Island. There appear to be only four pilots. The remainder are undoubtedly ground crew, standing in front of a trophy. During this period, squadrons competed in various air shows, races, and gunnery-bombing competitions.

**RED DEVILS**. The original Red Devil squadron was activated on September 1, 1925, at NAS North Island as Fighting Plane Squadron 3M (VF-3M). The first Red Devil aircraft was the Vought VE-7SF that came into the Marine Corps inventory in 1921. The line of planes shown here are F4B-4s, with pilots and ground crew standing by for inspection. Like all squadrons, VF-3M had several name changes and eventually became VMFA-232 and flying F/A-18 Hornets at MCAS Miramar.

**VMS-2**. VMS-2 squadron was formerly VO-8M, and Observation Squadron I before that. This squadron photograph was taken in the late 1930s.

**FORMATION FLIGHT.** This formation flight consists of five Curtiss Observation aircraft (OC-1s and OC-2s) from NAS North Island. The nearest aircraft has the Utility squadron logo (VJ-7M) on the tail, while the second aircraft has the VO-8M or VMS-2 Ace of Spades logo on its tail.

**RED DEVIL F6C-4.** This F6C-4 (F=fighter; 6=model; C=Curtiss, the manufacturer; and 4=version) has the Red Devil logo on the vertical stabilizer. The Red Devils received the F6C-4 in 1930, replacing the FB-5. This series of aircraft began use of air-cooled radial engines as Navy fighters.

RED DEVILS IN A STACK. The Boeing F4B-4s are probably the most famous of the Boeing fighters used by the Marine Corps. This stack clearly has the Red Devil logo on the tail. Also, the enlarged headrest was added to the last 45 F4B-4s built, and it included a life raft. The F4B-3 and 4 had a 550-horsepower engine. By 1939, the Marine Corps had 198 pilots and 1,142 enlisted men serving in aviation, up from 46 pilots and 756 enlisted men in the early 1920s.

CAMP KEARNY BLIMP OPERATIONS. Although used as an auxiliary airfield by everyone from Charles Lindbergh (testing the *Spirit of St. Louis*) to Army, Navy, and Marine Corps pilots from North Island, Camp Kearny did not receive much notoriety until the enormous blimps of the 1930s started arriving. On May 11, 1932, the 785-foot USS *Akron* landed at the camp. The *Akron* was a flying aircraft carrier able to carry five Curtiss Sparrow Hawk fighters to deploy in its defense or against the enemy.

AIRBORNE AIRCRAFT CARRIER. The most innovative feature of the USS *Akron* class of blimp was its ability to carry, launch, and recover five aircraft. In the belly of the blimp, a 75- by 60- by 16-foot hangar carried the aircraft. A T-shaped opening in the floor allowed a trapeze to be lowered that could release and recover the aircraft from skyhooks.

**F9C-2 Sparrow Hawk.** An F9C-2 catches the skyhook lowered by the USS *Macon*, another airborne aircraft carrier that landed at Camp Kearny in 1934. The USS *Akron* crashed at sea on the East Coast, losing 73 of its 76 crewman, and the *Macon* crashed on the West Coast shortly thereafter, but only lost 2 of a crew of 81. These crashes ended the rigid-blimp, airborne-carrier concept, but smaller non-rigid blimps continued to fly in the Navy until the 1950s.

**Blimp Landing.** Blimps never actually land; they fly very low to attach to a manned mooring mast that is towed to a hangar or parking area. The sailor on top of this mooring mast had to use caution to ensure that the blimp had grounded itself before he touched the line and secured it to the mooring mast. A blimp builds up a great amount of static electricity that discharges into the first thing on the ground it touches.

# *Three*

# THE 1940S AT CAMP KEARNY-MIRAMAR

Marine Corps Aviation Base Kearny Mesa, San Diego originated March 1, 1943, and was redesignated Marine Corps Air Depot Miramar (MCAD) September 2, 1943. MCAD Miramar served as the West Coast depot for Marine aviation units headed for combat in the Pacific. MCAD was responsible for equipping personnel, providing supplies and equipment to squadrons, physical examinations and administrative support, and whatever it took to launch a squadron into a combat environment. The other half of the base, Naval Auxiliary Air Station, Camp Kearny contained the runways, hangars, and control tower, and was operated by the U.S. Navy. The primary Navy mission was training aircrews in the Consolidated PB4Y Liberators that were built in San Diego. In January 1944, the first PB4Y crash occurred, on takeoff, killing the 13-man crew. In May 1944, the base lost three PB4Ys and their crews: one crashed on approach, three days later one had a midair collision with a F4F, and a week later one crashed into a base building, killing 36 men in 10 days. During World War II, both sides of Camp Kearny operated at capacity supporting the war in the Pacific; station personnel numbered 611 officers and 4076 enlisted men in mid-1944. In 1946, the base was redesignated MCAS Miramar, but only 13 months later the Marines relocated to MCAS El Toro and Miramar once again became Navy Auxiliary Air Station. After the war ended, the base was used as a separations center, returning 25,000 personnel to civilian life. In 1949, the Navy began a program to improve the runways and the base, and establish Miramar as a Master Jet Base.

**AERIAL VIEW.** Here is an aerial view of early Miramar runways looking toward the west. The numbers on Runway 24 are in clear view.

**GATE SIGN.** The gate sign shows some of the confusion that existed during the early days of Camp Kearny. The Marine Corps operated on one side of the base, originally called Marine Corps Aviation Base Kearny Mesa, while the Navy operated on the other end of the base and called their side Navy Auxiliary Air Station (Auxiliary to NAS North Island) Camp Kearny. The Marines changed their name to Marine Corps Air Depot Miramar to avoid confusion.

**CAMP KEARNY, GATE.** In this 1940s view of the East Gate to Camp Kearny, the station theater is visible in the background.

**COLORS.** At 0800 hours, the flag was raised while the band played the national anthem. Everyone in the military and most civilians who hear the music stop, face the flag, come to attention, and salute or place their hands over their hearts. For many, raising the flag in the morning stirs up deep patriotic feelings, and the few minutes it takes to complete the ceremony presents a time to reflect and give thanks for the freedoms and liberties won by America's military.

**EARLY CONSTRUCTION.** The early days at Marine Corps Aviation Depot (MCAD) were hectic and often chaotic. From a dirt mesa covered with scrub brush and chaparral wildlife, the Marines built a fully functional aviation support base in only months. Construction of new buildings, roads, train corridors, barracks, mess halls, clubs, and everything else needed by thousands of transiting Marines was conducted at a wartime pace.

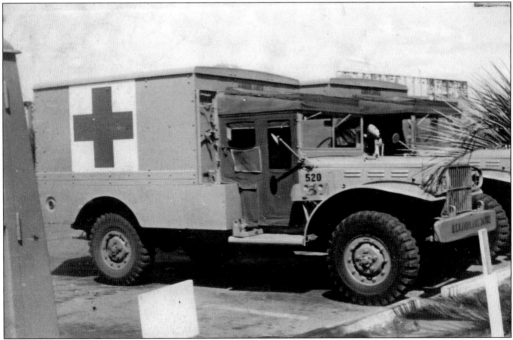

**AMBULANCE.** A 1940s ambulance parks in front of the Camp Kearny dispensary.

**MARINE AIRCRAFT GROUP 15, OPERATIONS.** Within a week of the attack on Pearl Harbor, VMJ-152 departed Quantico, arriving at Camp Kearny on December 14, 1942, to establish an air-transport training facility for the USMC. The engineers laid a concrete landing strip suitable for DC-3s and C-46s, and the training program was operational in record time. VMJ-152 quickly expanded into several squadrons and was redesignated Marine Aircraft Group 15 on March 1, 1942. Here the squadron duty officer mans the phones and the radios during flight operations.

**MARINE AIRCRAFT GROUP 15, FLIGHT OPERATIONS BOARD.** During a training day, dozens of flights are scheduled, delayed for maintenance reasons, rescheduled, and sometimes canceled. Pilots come and go with a million questions, checking weather, filing flight plans, and complaining to maintenance about their planes not having any fuel. On this schedule, the only names that can be read are McKay and Kelso, who are to fly an R5C-1.

**SUPPLY SQUADRON NO. 5.** During the buildup for war in the Pacific, few groups were more important than the supply squadrons. They provided everything an individual or a squadron needed to deploy to the combat theater. "Beans, bullets, Band-Aids, and bombs," as the saying goes, were just the tip of the supply iceberg.

**THE MASCOT.** The expression on the face of Supply Squadron No. 5's mascot is reflective of the grit and determination Marines manifested during the entire war.

MARINE CORPS AVIATION DEPOT BAND. The big-band sound was in full swing during the 1940s, and most bases had a band. Marine Corps Base Camp Lejuene, North Carolina, had an all-female reserve band. These bands were very talented and provided great entertainment for all who attended their performances, especially if one knew how to jitterbug.

MIRAMAR POST OFFICE. The top line on the sign says "Depot Post Office," but the second line appears to say Marine Corps Air Station Miramar, indicating that this picture was taken after the Marines took over the entire base in 1946.

**MIRAMAR BASKETBALL TEAM.** Most Marine Corps bases have an extensive intramural sports program, and during the 1940s Marine Corps football teams played against college teams. This picture shows the 1943–1944 Miramar basketball team.

**WOMEN'S RESERVE.** In 1943, the Women's Reserve (WR) was reactivated and thousands of female Marines descended onto Marine Corps bases all over the country. Women served with distinction during the war, performing every non-combat job possible. Their contributions to the war effort have often been ignored, but their service speaks for itself.

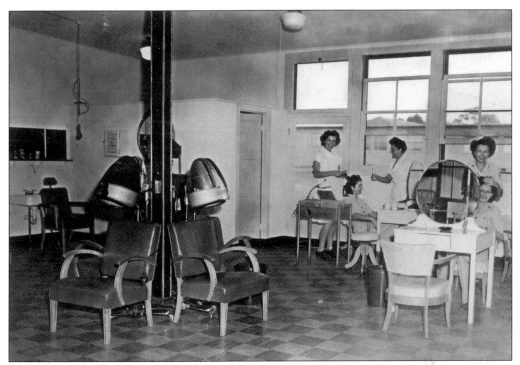

**MIRAMAR BEAUTY SALON.** One of the first things that had to be built upon the arrival of the WR was the base beauty salon. It wasn't fancy, but it served its purpose.

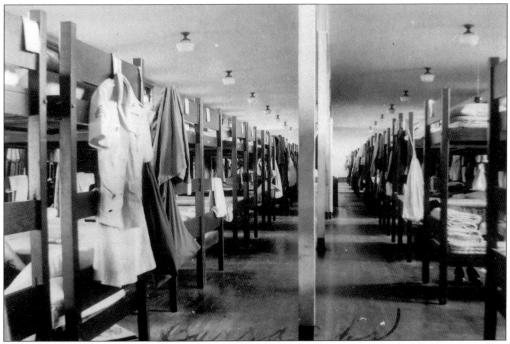

**WOMEN'S BARRACKS.** Men and women used the old squad bay-type barracks during this period. Bunk beds and a foot locker under the beds comprised one's universe in those days. If lucky, a Marine was permitted a wall locker, but usually not until a couple stripes were earned.

**WOMEN'S RESERVE POST OFFICE.** The WR had their own compound at Miramar, providing an element of convenience as well as security. Two reservists drive the mail cart from the main post office to the WR post office where the mail is sorted.

**WOMEN'S RESERVE BOXING MATCH.** Women also had a full schedule of intramural sports. Here a boxing match between female competitors looks fairly serious.

**MOTOR TRANSPORT SECTION.** The Motor Transport Section also provided valuable services. During the 1940s, and especially during the war, privately owned vehicles were scarce, even if you had a Gas Ration Card. This is a picture of the Miramar Motor "T" section during 1944–1945.

**POST OFFICE "GANG."** Those working in the post office are among the most popular people on any base or in any unit. Mail call is right up there with chow time and TAPS as the most popular sounds heard. This crew of postal ladies served as the WR mail "gang" during 1944–1945.

**MIRAMAR GROCERY STORE.** During the war, Camp Kearny evolved into a full-service military facility providing a wide range of amenities and services to the Marines and Sailors who served there. In the 1940s, before the days of McDonalds and Wal-Mart, the grocery store was a big hit.

**WOMEN'S RESERVE BARRACKS AREA.** This view of the WR barracks area shows tennis courts on the right and reservists working on their tans behind the barracks.

**WOMEN'S RESERVE CLUB.** Each base usually had a variety of clubs broken down by rank. There was an Enlisted Club, an NCO Club, a Staff NCO Club, and an Officer's Club; the WRs had their own club as well. Here a group of reservists enjoy libations after work.

**MIRAMAR WOMEN'S RESERVE SOFTBALL TEAM.** You can tell by the uniforms these WRs took the game seriously. The large "M" on their uniform identified these reservists as Miramar's finest.

AIR GUNNERY INSTRUCTORS. This group served as aerial gunnery instructors at Miramar during 1944–1945.

NAVY NURSE CORPS. All medical services for the Marine Corps are provided by the U.S. Navy. This group photograph shows the Navy Nurses serving at Miramar in the mid-1940s. Nurses and Corpsmen are among the most revered members of the Navy for their courage and dedication taking care of sick or wounded Marines.

**NAVY CORPSMEN.** This is a group photograph of the Navy Corpsmen serving at Miramar in 1946.

**MIRAMAR STATION PERSONNEL.** This is a photograph of the Naval Auxiliary Air Station, Miramar personnel on October 17, 1947.

**Miramar Control Tower.** This picture was taken after the Marines departed for MCAS El Toro and the Navy took over control of Miramar in late 1947. During World War II, the early "war birds," as they are known, crowded the skies over Miramar. Each aircraft possessed a unique appearance and a unique sound. Some of those aircraft are depicted on later pages.

**F2A Brewster Buffalo.** The Brewster Aeronautical Corporation began construction of the XF2A-1 prototype in March 1936, delivering it to the Navy in January 1938 for testing. After numerous modifications, the XF2A-1 met flight test expectations with a speed of 304 miles per hour, at an altitude of 6,000 feet, and a climb rate of 2,750 feet per minute. The Navy officially accepted the aircraft in June 1938 and ordered production to begin on 54 F2A-1s, later to be called the Brewster Buffalo. (Courtesy FLAM.)

**SB2C HELLDIVER.** The SB2C Helldiver was not a popular aircraft with those who flew it, and it earned many derogatory names. The Navy ordered the first prototype in May 1939, which was completed by December 1940. Despite being untested with many lingering problems, the Navy ordered 370 aircraft almost three weeks before the prototype was finished. During flight-testing, during a dive-bombing run from 22,000 feet, the right wing and tail failed, sending the prototype spinning to the ground. (Courtesy FLAM.)

**F4F WILDCAT.** The Grumman F4F Wildcat served as the Navy–Marine Corps' primary fighter in the Pacific during the early days of World War II through the Guadalcanal campaign. Earning a reputation as a durable plane, the Wildcat also was a product of "Grumman Iron Works," who had a reputation for well-built aircraft. The Marine Corps received its first Wildcats in November 1941, only weeks before the attack on Pearl Harbor. (Courtesy FLAM.)

**SBD Dauntless.** The Dauntless became the most famous Navy–Marine Corps bomber of World War II. Although considered obsolete before the war began and scheduled for retirement, the Dauntless was the only U.S. aircraft to participate in all five carrier-versus-carrier battles in the Pacific during World War II. In 1942, the bomber sunk more enemy vessels than all the other aircraft combined. The SBD-1 was armed with two forward-firing .50-caliber machine guns, a .30-caliber machine gun in the backseat position, and could carry a 1,600-pound centerline bomb with a 100-pound depth charge under each wing. (Courtesy FLAM.)

**TBF/M Avenger.** The Navy contracted for two prototype TBF-1s in April 1940, and by August 1941 the first one was flying. When the attack on Pearl Harbor occurred, the TBF received its name, the Avenger. By June 1942, six Avengers entered the Battle of Midway, but only one returned and it was seriously damaged. The Avenger was designed as a torpedo bomber, but could also drop mines and depth charges. Affectionately known as the "Turkey" because it was the largest single-engine bomber of its time, the Avenger was one of the great aircraft of World War II. (Courtesy FLAM.)

**F4U CORSAIR, "WHISTLING DEATH."** In June 1941, the Navy awarded Vought Aircraft Company a contract to build the F4U-1 Corsair, and 5,559 were eventually constructed. The manufacturers and the Navy knew they had a winner during the prototype test trials when the Corsair flew a record airspeed of 405 miles per hour. However, problems during the aircraft carrier trials forced the F4U-1 to temporarily become a land-based fighter. VMF-124 was the first Marine squadron to fly the Corsair in combat. The plane's unique aerodynamics in a dive produced a sound known by the Japanese as "Whistling Death." (Courtesy FLAM.)

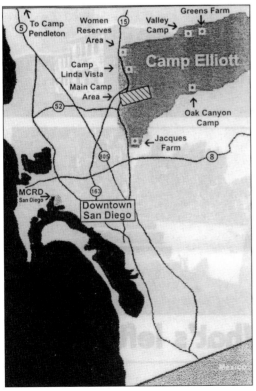

**CAMP ELLIOT MAP.** Camp Elliot, previously called Camp Holcomb in 1934 after the commandant, was formally designated on June 14, 1940, as Camp Elliot after another officer, the 10th Marine Corps commandant. In September 1942, Camp Elliot became the home of the Fleet Marine Force Training Center, West Coast. Camp Elliot's mission was to train combat replacements for ground units. This included, but was not limited to, the parachute school, artillery training, machine-gun training, basic weapons training, and small-unit tactics.

**AERIAL VIEW.** This view of Camp Elliot shows the extensive barracks complex and supporting buildings to maintain the training center at Camp Elliot. The camp eventually expanded to over 26,000 acres but was still too small to handle all the Marines that needed training.

**MAIN GATE.** This view of the Camp Elliot main gate shows some of the many barracks and the red and white checkered water towers that are a local landmark.

**FLAG RAISING.** Each morning, at 0800 hours, on every Marine Corps base around the world, the flag is ceremoniously raised. Three Marines and a bugler stand ready to raise the flag over Camp Elliot.

**9TH MARINE REGIMENT.** In March of 1942, construction began to build Marine Corps Base Camp Pendleton. During the summer of that year, the 9th Marine Regiment, located at Camp Elliot, marched from Camp Elliot to Camp Pendleton to become the first Marine unit to be stationed at Camp Pendleton.

**BAYONET TRAINING.** Marines train on the bayonet course at Camp Elliot.

**BOARDING A TRANSPORT FOR PARACHUTE TRAINING.** Marines trained at the Camp Elliot Parachute School until Camp Gillespie, near El Cajon, California, became available.

**PARACHUTE TRAINING.** The skies over Camp Elliot are filled with parachutes from Marines learning the skill at the parachute school.

**MACHINE-GUN TRAINING.** Marines train on heavy caliber, water-cooled machine guns.

**FLAMETHROWER TRAINING.** This Marine, in full protective gear, prepares to shoot a flamethrower. This could be a dangerous weapon not only for the enemy, but for the shooter as well. If the wind is blowing in the wrong direction the man behind the trigger can get a back blast in the face.

*Four*

# NAVY DAYS

Naval Air Station Miramar was dedicated as Mitscher Field in 1955 to honor Admiral M. A. Mitscher, USN, who gained notoriety leading Task Force 58 in World War II against Japanese forces in the Pacific. Task Force 58 was credited with sinking a thousand Japanese ships and destroying the Japanese Air Force.

Conceived in 1949 as an ideal location for a Master Jet Air Station, funds followed in 1951 to upgrade station facilities, and on April 1, 1952, Miramar was designated as a Naval Air Station. Gradually the base improved and expanded, adding a bachelor enlisted quarters, a recreation hall, a photography lab in 1958, and doubling in size in 1961 upon acquisition of Camp Elliot or East Miramar. Also in 1961, Miramar became the support base and home station for all West Coast Navy fighter squadrons, earning the name Fightertown. In 1965, CNO designated the Commander, Fleet Air Miramar as the senior command at Miramar. The Top Gun (Fighter Weapons School) arrived at Miramar in 1969 to train the "best of the best" fighter pilots. In July 1973, with the addition of the "early warning squadrons," the senior command at Miramar became Commander, Fighter-Airborne Early Warning Wing Pacific Fleet. By 1973, NAS Miramar was established as the Navy's training site for all F-14 Tomcat and E2C Hawkeye aircrews destined for Pacific Fleet squadrons. In the 1980s, the movie *Top Gun* was a box-office hit and the Miramar Officer's Club became famous around the world. By 1993, NAS Miramar conducted an average of 265,000 takeoffs and landings per year. In 1994, the first Marine squadrons arrived to begin the transition from NAS Miramar to MCAS Miramar.

**C-117 SKY MASTER, MIRAMAR.** The C-117 Sky Master was one of the greatest aircraft designs of all time. Originally known as the Douglas DC-3, it became one of the world's most popular transport aircraft between 1936 and 1941. The Navy purchased its first DC-3 in 1941, and many are still flying in the civilian aviation community to this day. During the early days of World War II, variants of the DC-3 used Miramar extensively and performed exemplary duty resupplying Marines during the World War II "island hoping" campaigns in the Pacific and evacuating wounded. (Courtesy FLAM.)

**HANGAR CONSTRUCTION.** Congress devised the Woods Plan to realign and upgrade certain military facilities following World War II. Naval Air Station Miramar was once offered to the City of San Diego for $1 because the Navy wanted to close Miramar. But in July 1949, under the Woods Plan, Miramar was designated as a Master Jet Base. Within 14 months, federal funds became available to begin a major construction and rehabilitation effort. Miramar was the first and largest Master Jet Base at the time. On April 1, 1952, Miramar was redesignated as Naval Air Station Miramar. This October 1952 photograph shows the hangar construction.

AIRCRAFT PARKING AREA. New construction at Miramar continued throughout the 1950s. By 1958, many projects had been completed, including new enlisted men's barracks, a recreation hall, and one of the most modern photographic laboratories in the Armed Forces. This January 1953 photograph shows work-in-progress expanding the aircraft parking areas.

BARRACKS CONSTRUCTION. This May 1957 photograph shows work in progress on the second phase of the enlisted barracks projects.

**CHIEF'S CLUB CONSTRUCTION.** The Navy's Chief Petty Officer's Club is a place of high tradition and often strange and mystical nautical enigmas. This photograph shows the new club nearing completion in the late 1950s.

**NOSE HANGARS AND MAINTENANCE AREA, OCTOBER 1964.** This area, called Splinterville, provided nose hangars and auxiliary maintenance buildings for flight-line level maintenance. During hot summers or rainy San Diego winters, these facilities provided top-level maintenance support and a little protection from the elements.

**MITSCHER FIELD.** In 1955, Naval Air Station Miramar was dedicated as Mitscher Field to honor Adm. M. A. Mitscher, USN, who commanded Task Force 58 in the Pacific during World War II. His force was credited with sinking 1,000 ships and virtually destroying the Japanese Air Force. In one battle, planes from his carriers downed 402 enemy planes and only lost 27 American planes. A "full speed ahead"–style commander, he was respected and admired by his subordinates.

**THE ADMIRAL'S RIDE.** Whenever VIPs showed up at NAS Miramar, the base commander always rendered the highest military honors and provided the VIPs with a tour of the flight line in a custom Navy flight-line vehicle.

**NAVAL AIR STATION MIRAMAR LOGO.** In 1961, Miramar became the support base and home station for fighter squadrons only. It was not long after that the name "Fightertown" began appearing on buildings and letterheads. This logo is loaded with symbolism ranging from the globe, the Pacific Ocean, and the Naval Aviator Wings spanning the ocean to the eagles topping the logo.

**FIGHTERTOWN LOGO.** Miramar's new name of Fightertown could be found just about anywhere on the base, including on the tail of this aircraft.

**USS ORISKANY CV34**. Aviation in the U.S. Navy is all about aircraft carrier operations and deployments to places far, far away. This 1968 photograph shows a carrier with a variety of aircraft on deck, including the F4 Phantom II, the A4 Skyhawk, the A3 Sky Warrior, the AD Skyraider, the E2C Hawkeye, and a couple of helicopters.

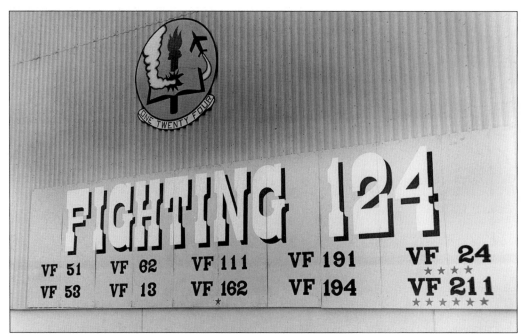

**FIGHTING VF-124.** VF-124 was commissioned in 1958 at NAS Moffett Field before relocating in 1961 to NAS Miramar. During the 1960s, VF-124 served as the squadron that trained pilots and aircrews to fly the F8 Crusader. In 1970, VF-124 was designated as a training squadron to introduce the F-14 Tomcat to the fleet. By 1976, VF-124's training program was in full operation and fleet replacement crews were being trained, as well as providing training for Iranian pilots. By 1978, VF-124 had trained 526 aircrews and 7,600 maintenance personnel. (Courtesy FLAM.)

**F8U-2 CRUSADER VF-124.** As the only F8 Crusader training squadron in the Navy, VF-124 is said to have the distinction of training the "last of the gunfighters." The F8 Crusader was an extremely complex aircraft and one of the world's fastest jets, operating near twice the speed of sound and at over 50,000 feet. The F8 was the last true "single-seat" fighter plane in service during its day and was extremely effective. (Courtesy FLAM.)

**COMMANDER FLEET AIR LOGO.** On July 15, 1965, the Commander, Fleet Air Miramar (COMFAIRMIRAMAR) was designated as the senior command on board at Miramar. On July 1, 1973, the COMFAIRMIRAMAR added the airborne early warning squadrons to its command and was redesignated by the Chief of Naval Operations as Commander, Fighter-Airborne Early Warning Wing U.S. Pacific Fleet (COMFITAEWWINGPAC).

**F4 PHANTOM II, VF-143 MIRAMAR BASE OPERATIONS.** VF-143 originated at Naval Air Station Alameda, California, as a reserve squadron flying F4U Corsairs in 1949. Activated twice to participate in the Korean War, the squadron transitioned through a variety of aircraft and designations. They flew the F9F Panther, the F3H Demon, then transitioned to the F4 Phantom II, and eventually moved to the F-14 Tomcat. After spending many years at Miramar, VF-143 relocated to NAS Oceana in 1976. (Courtesy FLAM.)

**ADMINISTRATIVE BUILDING.** The base administrative building, pictured here in the late 1960s, was a mini-landmark aboard Miramar for a couple reasons. It was one of the buildings that almost everyone visited at one time or another for a variety of administrative needs, and it was one of the older buildings on the base.

**SATELLITE CLUB.** The Satellite Club was available to enlisted personnel of the rank E-5 and E-6. Like most clubs, the Satellite Club provided ambiance, entertainment, and libation, and a great place to relieve stress to foster the esprit de corps common in the naval service.

**CPO MESS.** The CPO mess is seen here as those who served at Miramar and who utilized the club's services will remember it. Open to active duty, retired, and reserve enlisted ranks of E-7–E-9 and their guests, the CPO mess was used extensively for parties, weddings, ceremonies, and for morale building.

**NAVAL AIR RESERVE HEADQUARTERS.** The Naval Air Reserve Center, Miramar, previously called Naval Air Reserve Detachment (NARDET), was commissioned on July 1, 1979. It was the largest air reserve center in the Navy, supporting many flying squadrons, augmentation units, and staff units by providing all administrative and operational support.

**CHAPEL.** The base chapel gets much more business than one might imagine, especially during times of war or long deployments. Active duty, reserves, and dependents use the multi-faith facility for much more than their spiritual needs. Weddings, baptisms, choir practice, Bible instruction, and counseling are provided by the Chaplain Corps.

**ENLISTED DINING FACILITY.** One of the many great things that can be said about the Navy is that they have great mess halls. Even when the other services were eating mystery meat and drinking bug juice, the Navy provided a good bill of fare.

CHOW LINE. Walking through the "chow" line has always carried with it an almost ritualistic or ceremonial aura. Greeting the friendly and cheerful cooks three times a day, exchanging pleasantries while being served gourmet delicacies, not only aided digestion but also set the mood for the rest of the day. Navy mess halls very often had the walls painted with murals of tropical islands and seminude native girls fluttering about.

THE BARN. A great recreational facility for naval personnel, the barn was filled with pool tables and pinball machines. When the Marines repossessed Miramar, their idea of recreation was to replace the pool tables and pinball machines with stair-climbers, stationary bicycles, and treadmills.

**ENLISTED CLUB.** The Enlisted Club had two parts that consisted of the Barrier, open to non-rated personnel, and the Jet Stream side, catering to noncommissioned petty officers. The clubs were open seven days a week and provided a variety of entertainment options, including bingo.

**OFFICERS' CLUB.** The Miramar Officers' Club gained notoriety and fame after the movie *Top Gun* hit the silver screen. Maverick, Goose, and Ice Man imitators abounded during post "danger zone" times. Swaggers and impromptu serenades of oldies songs by Navy pilots became so prolific that at one point a not-so-prominent U.S. senator stepped in, demanding a cooling-off period. When the Marines took control of the "danger zone" in the mid-1990s, they redecorated the club in Marine photographs and memorabilia, offering a great place to enjoy the ambience of a historical setting.

**NAVY EXCHANGE.** One of any sailor's high points, especially on weekends, is a visit to the base exchange. Although it is little more than a Walmart combined with a food court, it provides a place to purchase many of life's daily necessities, but also a social setting in which to meet friends and relieve stresses.

**DRILL TEAM.** The Miramar award-winning "X" Division Honor Guard poses for a photograph.

**AVIATION PHYSIOLOGY BUILDING.** Aviation physiology is a unique science that requires intimate familiarity by all aviators. The physical and medical effects of altitude and pressure changes on the body, G-forces, the science of day and night vision, and a myriad of other factors are taught by aviation physiology professionals hoping to keep pilots alive. One of the best lessons discussed was an aviator who went scuba diving in the morning and flying in the afternoon. After passing somewhere through 10,000 feet he started getting the bends.

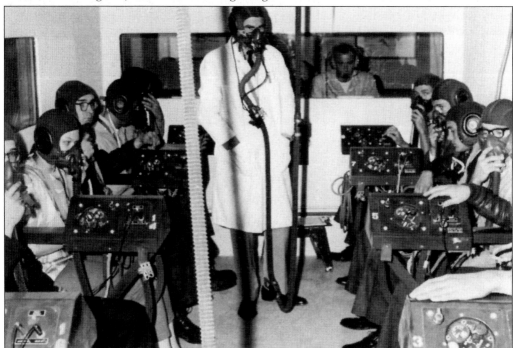

**HIGH-ALTITUDE PRESSURE CHAMBER.** Before anyone can fly, or even ride, in high-performance military aircraft, they must pass a series of tests administered by the aviation physiology department. The high-altitude pressure chamber introduces aviators to changing pressures, the concept of blocked nasal passages, and the effects of diminishing oxygen levels. A favorite video of students shows how flight surgeons clear a sinus block with a long needle up the nose into the sinus cavity.

**WATER SURVIVAL.** Water survival training is among the most challenging aspects of naval aviation training. Parachuting into a cold, empty ocean at night usually is a life-threatening experience. Without excellent training, the downed aircrew has little chance of survival. If they manage to get into the life raft, surviving until they are rescued is the next step. Learning proper use of the contents of the survival kit, signaling devices, and drinking-water rationing aid the chances of survival dramatically.

**LIFE RAFT.** Imagine falling from 10,000 feet into the ocean and trying to climb out of a cold, stormy ocean on a dark night with ten foot swells, into a little raft dressed in a flight suit, helmet and boots. All this happens while wearing a G-suit and survival vest, with a parachute strapped on back trying to drag the pilot under the water. It takes practice.

**ENGINE SHOP.** Among the most important departments on any air base is the engine shop. Few components on an aircraft are more important than the engine and are in the trust of the most skilled professionals on the base. Although modern jet engines have been perfected to yield thousands of hours of top performance, maintenance and inspections are required to ensure the highest and safest production. Engine mechanics are among the least heralded but most crucial members of any unit.

**FLIGHT EQUIPMENT DEPARTMENT.** The flight equipment department is best known as the place where pilots get those Tom Cruise sunglasses or those leather flight jackets. However, flight equipment personnel do much more, including everything from maintaining and packing parachutes, to servicing and packing survival equipment in individual vests, life rafts, or aircraft emergency equipment. The extensive range of equipment now worn by aircrews requires top-level maintenance or they become ineffective.

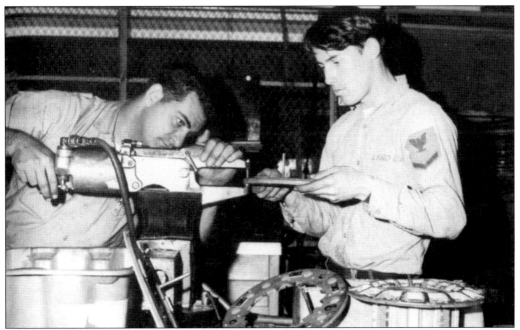

MACHINE SHOP. On any given day, at any given air base, dozens of aircraft are down for maintenance and/or servicing. Often a part, a shim, an O-ring, or some very small item is preventing that multi-million dollar aircraft from flying its mission. Just as often a skilled machine shop operator can produce that needed part in anywhere from a few minutes to a few hours, saving the day for the flight-scheduling officer.

SIMULATOR TRAINING. Simulator training is at the top of the list of beneficial training for naval aviators. A pilot can practice multiple emergency situations in a simulator, over and over again, preparing for the time when the emergency is real.

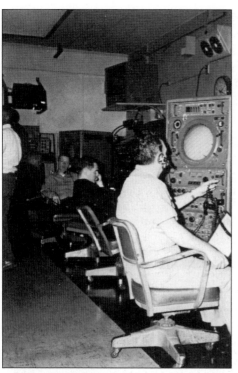

RADAR. Any pilot who has ever flown to an airport when the weather was bad, or with a broken aircraft, or was simply lost, will attest to how much the folks who work in the radar section of air traffic control are appreciated. Most pilots have had their day saved on numerous occasions by skilled and conscientious radar operators who provide clear and calm guidance, vectors, or updates during moments of shear terror in the cockpit.

BOMB STACK. One would think that working in the ordnance department shuffling bombs around the area all day would be a dangerous job. It is, but somehow properly trained personnel perform miraculously arming and de-arming ordnances and loading and unloading aircraft with very few accidents or mistakes.

**MARINE DETACHMENT.** The Marine detachment on board NAS Miramar served as perimeter security and immediate response for emergencies as part of the NAS North Island Marine Barracks. Marines have a long history of protecting the Navy, serving as security on naval vessels, and generally providing role models for naval personnel. The Navy–Marine Corps relationship mirrors the British model and dates to the Marine Corps birth in 1775.

**MARINE ON GATE.** Many a sailor returning from liberty dreaded the mandatory identification card check with the Marine gate sentry. The Navy and Marine Corps have always had a "special" relationship, each holding the other in the highest esteem.

**CONTROL TOWER.** Managing a Navy–Marine Corps airfield is primarily the responsibility of the Air Field Operations department. It has many sections including, but not limited to the crash, fire, rescue department, the visiting aircraft line, the control tower personnel, and the air traffic control system. With as many as 1,000 landings and takeoffs a day and up to a couple hundred arrested landings a year, the operations department has its hands full.

**ADMIRALS EXAM.** Two naval aviators are studying for their promotion examination. Based on their obvious studiousness, these men are destined for great achievement and high rank in the Navy.

**CRASH INTO HANGAR.** A horrible accident occurred at NAS Miramar in December 1969. An F8J Crusader approached for an emergency landing when the aircraft's controls failed on short final. The pilot had to eject, and the pilot-less aircraft turned and crashed into Hangar 1. (Courtesy FLAM.)

**SMOLDERING WRECKAGE.** The F8J Crusader crashed into Hangar 1's north bay, bursting into flames and causing the fuel tanks of other aircraft parked in the hangar to explode. At the end of the day, 12 military and civilians working in the hangar lost their lives. In addition to the lost Crusader, five other Phantom II's were destroyed and left $20 million worth of damage to the hangar. Courageous efforts from firefighters kept the disaster from claiming more lives. (Courtesy FLAM.)

**VF-121, Flight of Phantoms over Miramar.** At the time of this photograph, VF-121 was one of the squadrons permanently based ashore at NAS Miramar. It was one of the largest Navy fighter squadrons that had the mission of training combat-ready aircrews and aviation maintenance personnel, developing and reviewing tactics, and updating standardization procedures (NATOPS). Over the course of time, two of their most prominent alumni were Lt. R. F. Gordon (setting a speed record) and astronaut Cdr. Pete Conrad (Apollo 12 lunar module pilot).

**F-14 Tomcat over Miramar.** The F-14 Tomcat was the Navy's supersonic, long-range fighter aircraft, providing sophisticated detection and tracking capabilities with maneuverability and speed. Manufactured by Grumman Aircraft and first introduced in 1973, the Tomcat is manned by a pilot and a radar intercept officer. The F-14 is armed with the Phoenix Missile System, the Sidewinder, and Sparrow Missiles, as well as the M61 cannon.

# Five

# 3RD MARINE AIRCRAFT WING (3DMAW)

Commissioned during World War II on November 10, 1942, at MCAS Cherry Point, North Carolina, the 3dMAW began with 13 officers, 25 enlisted men, and one aircraft. During that war, the 3dMAW fulfilled the role of a training and support wing, preparing squadrons and personnel for deployment to the Pacific. In 1944, the wing was deployed to Hawaii in support of the final phases of the war. At the end of the war, the 3dMAW was decommissioned but was reactivated in 1952 in support of the Korean War, operating from MCAS Miami, Florida. In September 1955, the 3dMAW relocated to MCAS El Toro, California, later supporting the Vietnam War and Desert Storm. In 1998, El Toro closed and the 3dMAW relocated once again to MCAS Miramar. In the fall of 2002, the 3dMAW began support of IMEF forces liberating Iraq. Throughout the 3dMAW's history, it has commanded some of the most courageous and famous flying squadrons in the Marine Corps. The VMFA-232 Red Devils is one of the Marine Corps oldest squadrons, activated on September 1, 1925, and served at North Island, California, during the 1920s and 1930s. The VMA-211 Wake Island Avengers were part of the famous defense of Wake Island during the first days of World War II. Eventually, the entire 211 detachment was either killed or captured when the Japanese overran Wake Island. HMM-161 is the Marine Corps first and oldest tactical helicopter squadron, standing up in September 1951 and defining early assault helicopter operations. The 3dMAW is comprised of many such units rich in heritage and courage.

**HOME OF THE 3RD MARINE AIRCRAFT WING.** The headquarters building is home to not only the commanding general and his staff, but also to the staff sections that coordinate much of the training, administrative support, logistical support, and wing-level maintenance support. During times of war, when squadrons are regularly deploying to and from the combat theater, the wing headquarters is a very busy place.

**BAND.** The 3d MAW Band was established for service during World War II. Soon after it ended, the band was deactivated and its members were sent to serve in Marine units in China and at MCAS Ewa, Hawaii. In 1952, the Third Marine Aircraft Wing Band was officially reactivated at MCAS Miami, Florida in support of the Korean Conflict, using Marine musicians returning from China and members of the Second Marine Aircraft Wing Band. (Courtesy USMC.)

**BAND MEMORIAL.** The 3dMAW Band Memorial is a tribute honoring and in remembrance of the 4th Marines Band, known as the "Last China Band." Forty-eight of the musicians from the 4th Marine Regiment Band fought, died, or became POWs during the siege of Bataan and Corregidor during World War II in 1942.

**MARINE AIRCRAFT GROUP 16 (MAG-16) HEADQUARTERS.** MAG-16 was formed March 1, 1952, at Santa Ana, California, consisting of eight units. Through the years, many other helicopter squadrons have joined MAG-16. Units of MAG-16 have participated in numerous conflicts, exercises, and operations from the Korean War and the Vietnam War, to Operations Desert Shield/Desert Storm and Operation Iraqi Freedom. Today MAG-16 is made up of 10 units.

**MAG-16 LOGO.** MAG-16 and its units have provided aircraft support and transportation for visiting U.S. dignitaries and celebrities, including the president of the United States, the secretary of defense, the secretary of the Navy, the commandant of the Marine Corps, and movie stars. MAG-16 supports the community with static displays, raising money for the unfortunate, visiting the sick, and providing food and medical care for victims of natural disasters.

**HMH-361 FLYING TIGERS.** HMH-361 is one of the Marine Corps' oldest helicopter squadrons, created in February 1952 at Marine Corps Air Facility (Helicopter) Santa Ana. A squadron with a rich history, 361 participated in atomic testing in Desert Rock, Nevada, and at the Bikini Islands in the South Pacific during the 1950s, and was one of the first Marine helicopter squadrons to deploy to Vietnam in 1963 and returned there in 1968. Over the years, 361 has flown the H-19, the H-34, the CH-53A and D model helicopters, and now the CH-53E Super Stallion, pictured here. (Courtesy George Dietsch.)

**HMH-361 FLYING TIGERS.** The Marine Corps used the H-19 Chickasaw helicopter during the Korean War to develop vertical assault tactics and strategies. However, by the war's end the need for a faster, more powerful helicopter was recognized. The H-34 entered service in 1955, and its versatility permitted the helicopter to perform a variety of missions for all branches of the service. The H-34 became best known in Marine Corps circles during Operation SHU-FLY in Vietnam during the early 1960s. (Courtesy FLAM.)

**HMH-462 HEAVY HAULERS.** HMH-462 was reactivated as a helicopter squadron in 1957 at Marine Corps Air Facility (Helicopter) Santa Ana. The squadron flew the CH-37 Mojave, also known as the HR2S Deuce. In 1958, the squadron was involved with NASA's abort "recovery" test of the Mercury Space Capsule. In 1968, the squadron was deployed to Vietnam and was primarily involved with tactical retrieval of downed aircraft. Relocated to Okinawa, HMH-462 participated in Operation "Eagle Pull" and the evacuation of Phnom Pen in 1975. (Courtesy FLAM.)

**HMH-462 HEAVY HAULERS.** The CH-53E Sea Stallion began arriving at Marine Corps squadrons in the early 1980s. Although very similar in appearance to the CH53A/D models, the E model is almost a totally different aircraft. The A/D model's max gross weight was 42,000 pounds as opposed to the E model's max gross weight of 73,500 pounds. The E model has three engines at 4,380 shaft horsepower versus two for the A/Ds, and there are seven main rotor blades on the E model compared to six on the A/Ds. The Super Stallion is the true workhorse of the Marine Corps. (Courtesy CWO Crow.)

**HMH-465 Warhorse.** HMH-465 originated on December 1, 1981, as the first squadron on the West Coast to fly the CH-53E Super Stallion. The 1980s were well spent training in the new helicopter with its high performance capabilities. The squadron became proficient in night vision goggle operations, which include but are not limited to landing on ships, aerial refueling, and performing external lift operations, as well as long-range, low-level training simulating hostage or embassy extracts, and/or troop inserts. (Courtesy USN.)

**HMH-465 Warhorse.** HMH-465 was deployed to the Middle East during the Persian Gulf War, participating extensively in combat operations. In 2004, they left for the Middle East, again in support of Operation Iraqi Freedom. While the squadron is stationed at Miramar, it finds itself supporting Combined Arms Exercises at 29 Palms, California, and joining unit deployments to Okinawa. (Courtesy George Dietsch.)

**HMH-466 WOLFPACK.** The HMH-466 Wolfpack originated on November 30, 1984, as the second CH-53E Super Stallion squadron on the West Coast. Over the next decade, the Wolfpack earned many awards for outstanding maintenance, safety, and performance. HMH-466 has supported numerous Marine Expeditionary Unit deployments, including Operation Restore Hope in Somalia, and continues to be one of the Marine Corps finest Heavy Lift/Special Operations Capable squadrons. (Courtesy Wolfpack.)

**CREW CHIEF.** Crew chiefs in the Marine Corps must have the single most overworked and underappreciated job in the Marine Corps, and that's saying something. During the early days of helicopters, crew chiefs could easily average 18-hour days, often sleeping in, on, or under the "bird" at night and working and flying it all day. The Corps invented the 12-hour crew day to lighten the aircrew load, but for the crew chief all that means is that he can only fly 12 hours in a day, but work on the helicopter the other 12 hours. (Courtesy USN.)

**HMM-161 GREYHAWKS.** Originating at MCAS El Toro on January 15, 1951, and relocated to MCAF (H) Santa Ana in February 1951 with the new HRS-1 Chickasaw helicopter (later known as the H-19), HMM-161 became the first assault helicopter squadron to deploy troops in combat. This era gave birth to helicopter vertical assault tactics and strategies, forever changing the manner wars are fought. Among the helicopters greatest roles is medical evacuation, which has extended the average troops combat life manyfold. (Courtesy FLAM.)

**HMM-161 GREYHAWKS.** Although the primary mission of any combat assault helicopter squadron is offensive combat support, helicopters just as frequently find themselves performing logistical resupply missions. On many occasions, the only way to resupply forward positions has been via helicopters. Helicopter aircrews train rigorously to perfect external lifting skills and techniques. The crew chief in the helicopter's cabin provides input to the pilots as well as a ground support team to ensure a successful lift or delivery. (Courtesy FLAM.)

**HMM-163 RIDGERUNNERS.** The HMM-163 Ridgerunners originated in December 1951, earning their nickname from Japan's mountainous terrain during typhoon relief operations. In 1966, during the battle for Ashau Valley in Vietnam, an HMM-163 crew chief painted "evil eyes" on his H-34 helicopter (pictured above). According to local fishermen, the eyes warded off evil spirits and guaranteed a good catch. After the mission, this crew chief's helicopter had the fewest bullet holes. During the 1990s, HMM-163 served as the Aviation Combat Element (ACE) for four Special Operations Capable Marine Expeditionary Units (MEU(SOC)) on deployments to the Pacific and Central Command theaters. The squadron also participated in operations from the Horn of Africa to the Northern Arabian Gulf, including Operation "Fiery Vigil" in 1991. In 2001, HMM-163 and the 15th MEU landed in Afghanistan, 400 miles inland at Camp Rhino in support of Operation Enduring Freedom. (Both photographs courtesy FLAM.)

**HMM-165 White Knights.** HMM-165 White Knights were activated on July 1, 1965, at MCAS (H) Santa Ana. During its existence, HMM-165 has become the gypsies of the Marine helicopter community, receiving assignments around the world. From Santa Ana, it was deployed to Vietnam, then to Okinawa and back to Vietnam, to the Philippines, and then to Kaneohe Bay, Hawaii. A few years later it was deployed to Lebanon, then to the Gulf War before relocating to El Toro and finally ending up at MCAS Miramar. (Courtesy FLAM.)

**HMM-165 White Knights Landing in an LZ.** In January 2003, HMM-165 was deployed on the USS *Boxer* and cruised to the Arabian Gulf. After off-loading in Kuwait, the squadron was tasked with supporting Regimental Combat Team 1 (RCT-1) for the duration of Operation Iraqi Freedom. On the night of April 1, 2003, HMM-165 comprised the CH-46 element of Task Force 20, the special team that extracted prisoner of war, Army PFC Jessica Lynch. (Courtesy FLAM.)

**HMM-166 "Sea Elks."** On April 22, 1958, the Boeing Vertol 107 (later the CH-46) prototype made its first flight. The design was selected by the Marine Corps in February 1961, and the first CH-46A was flown on October 16, 1962. In early 1965 the first Marine Corps squadrons received the CH-46A. The helicopter entered combat in Vietnam almost immediately and served as a primary workhorse for the Marine Corps. (Courtesy USN.)

**HMM-166 Sea Elks.** HMM-166 (H=helicopter, M=Marine, M=medium) was the last CH-46 squadron commissioned in the Marine Corps, on September 13, 1985, at MCAS (H) Tustin, California. Over the next 20 years, the squadron supported many unique assignments, including the Alaskan pipeline oil spill in 1989, a deployment to Entebbe, Uganda, in 1994, and support of Operation Vigilant Warrior in Kuwait during the same year. (Courtesy FLAM.)

**MARINE AIRCRAFT GROUP, 39 LOGO.** MCAS Camp Pendleton dates to World War II, while MAG-39 history dates to the 1960s and the Vietnam War. MAG-39 was reactivated at Camp Pendleton in 1976 and slowly grew into a substantial Marine Aircraft Group in command of nine squadrons, including two training squadrons. Camp Pendleton air station has expanded to accommodate these squadrons with many new structures and a new control tower.

**MCAS CAMP PENDLETON LOGO.** The Camp Pendleton airfield was designated as an auxiliary landing field of MCAS El Toro in September 1942. It served primarily as a practice strip for nearby air stations, and an aircraft parking area for planes traveling to and from the combat theater. On September 1, 1978, the airfield was designated as a Marine Corps Air Facility and on March 24, 1987, it was upgraded to a MCAS. The airfield is named Munn Field in honor of Lt. Gen. Toby Munn, who was the first aviator to serve as commanding general of Camp Pendleton.

**HMLA-169 UH-1N**. MAG-39 has four HMLA (Helicopter Marine Light Attack) squadrons: HMLA-169, 267, 367, and 369. Each squadron is comprised of a combination of UH-1N Huey and AH-1W Cobra aircraft, providing superior flexibility in mission assignments. This UH-1N is "air taxiing" for takeoff. (Courtesy George Dietsch.)

**HMLA-169 UH-1N**. The UH-1N Huey may be the most famous and well-known helicopter of all time. It may also be one of the greatest aircraft designs, ranking with the DC-3 and the B-52 for longevity. Although initially conceived as a "utility" platform, the Huey does it all, ranging from VIP missions, attack roles, troop insert/extract missions (including rappelling and fast rope), as well as basic resupply. Few aircraft have been as versatile and reliable as the Huey. (Courtesy USN.)

**HMLA-367 COBRA.** A four-bladed version of the AH-1W, designated the AH-1Z, is under development; the addition of the extra blades dramatically improves the performance envelope of the AH-1W. The aircraft is also undergoing a cockpit reconfiguration to allow for easier copilot/gunner access to the night tactical systems (NTS). The upgrade of the AH-1W, including the new cockpit, is referred to as the Four Bladed AH-1W (4BW) and the upgrade of the UH-1N drive train is referred to as the Four Bladed UH-1N (4BN). (Courtesy George Dietsch.)

**HMMT-164 TRAINING SESSION.** HMM-164 was activated in July 1964 at MCAS (H) Santa Ana (later renamed Tustin) and received the CH-46 Sea Knight helicopter six months later. In 1966, HMM-164 was deployed to Vietnam for a three-and-a-half-year tour in Vietnam. The squadron relocated to Okinawa in 1969 and finally returned to Santa Ana in 1978. When the 1993 Base Closure Commission closed, MCAS Tustin HMM-164 relocated to Camp Pendleton and was redesignated HMMT-164, becoming a CH-46 training squadron. (Courtesy George Dietsch.)

**MARINE AIRCRAFT GROUP 11.** MAG-11's ancestral roots date to 1921 and rank it among the oldest Marine Corps aviation units. In August 1941, MAG-11 was commissioned as the Marine Corps's first aviation group with six tactical squadrons, and relocated from Quantico to the San Diego area serving as the Air-Defense Group. In October 1942, MAG-11 was deployed to the South Pacific in support of combat operations near the New Hebrides Islands and other notable combat operations. (Courtesy George Dietsch.)

**MAG 11 COLORS.** The Marine Aircraft Group 11 flag stands proud.

**VMFA-232 RED DEVILS.** Activated on September 1, 1925, at North Island, VMFA-232 is one of the oldest squadrons in the Marine Corps and enjoys some of the most colorful history. Flying during the Roaring Twenties and the Desperate Thirties, VMFA-232's predecessors helped lay the groundwork for the development of close air support, dive-bombing, and dog-fighting techniques that would be used throughout World War II. The squadron was deactivated at MCAD Miramar in 1945 after World War II but reactivated in 1948. (Courtesy FLAM.)

**VMFA-232 RED DEVILS.** On July 1, 1937, the squadron was redesignated as VMB-2, and in 1940 it received brand-new SBD-1 Dauntless aircraft. With war in the Pacific brewing, the squadron relocated to Ewa, Hawaii, and on July 1, 1941, it was redesignated again as Marine Scout Bombing Squadron 232 (VMSB-232). When the Japanese attacked Pearl Harbor, they destroyed 9 and seriously damaged 10 of the other 232 aircraft. After receiving replacement SBD-3s, VMSB-232 relocated to Guadalcanal. (Courtesy George Dietsch.)

**VMFA-242: THE BATS.** Activated as Marine Torpedo Bombing Squadron 242 on July 1, 1943, at El Centro, California, the squadron initially flew SNJs and SBDs, but within a month 242 received its first TBM and TBF Avengers. In January 1944, the squadron was deployed to the South Pacific engaging in combat operations against the Japanese. Returning to San Diego in November 1945, the squadron was deactivated. On October 1, 1960, 242 was reactivated as VMA-242 at Cherry Point, North Carolina, flying the A4D Skyhawk. (Courtesy FLAM.)

**VMFA-242: THE BATS.** In October 1964, 242 became the first Marine Corps squadron to fly the A6 Intruder. The A6 provided a much-needed, all-weather, close-air support capability for the Marine Corps. VMA(AW)-242 was deployed to Danang, Vietnam, in October 1966 and almost immediately began combat operations against enemy positions. In September 1970, VMA(AW)-242 relocated to MCAS El Toro. In 1990, 242 was redesignated as VMFA(AW)-242 and started transitioning from the A6 Intruder to the F/A-18 Hornet. (Courtesy George Dietsch.)

**VMFA-314 BLACK KNIGHTS.** VMF-314 was commissioned on October 1, 1943, at MCAS Cherry Point, North Carolina, and initially flew the F4U Corsair during World War II and participated in combat operations in the Okinawa campaign. Deactivated at the end of World War II, 314 was reactivated in 1952 with FG-1D Corsairs but, in December 1952, the Corsairs were replaced with the F9F Panther, their first jet aircraft. In June 1962, 314 was the first Marine squadron to receive the F4 Phantom II. (Courtesy FLAM.)

**VMFA-314 BLACK KNIGHTS.** The F/A-18 is an all-weather fighter and attack aircraft. The single-seat F/A-18 Hornet is the nation's first strike-fighter. It was designed for traditional strike applications, such as interdiction and close air support without compromising its fighter capabilities. The D model can carry up to 13,000 pounds of external ordnance on nine weapons stations at speeds up to Mach 1.8. (Courtesy George Dietsch.)

**VMFA-121 Green Knights.** VMF-121 was originally commissioned on June 24, 1941, at Quantico and joined combat operations in the South Pacific against the Japanese in early 1942. The squadron functioned as a reserve unit from 1946 to 1951 when it was activated for the Korean War and redesignated VMA-121 flying the AD-1 Skyraider. In the late 1950s, 121 received the A4C Skyhawk. In 1969, it transitioned once again to the A6 and flew Intruders until 1990 when it received the F/A-18 Hornet. (Courtesy FLAM.)

**VMFA-121 Green Knights.** The F/A-18 demonstrated its capabilities and versatility during Operation Desert Storm, shooting down enemy fighters and subsequently bombing enemy targets with the same aircraft on the same mission, and breaking all records for tactical aircraft availability, reliability, and maintainability. Hornets taking direct hits from surface-to-air missiles returned to base recovered successfully, were repaired quickly, and were flying again the next day, proving the aircraft's survivability. (Courtesy FLAM.)

**VMFA-323 DEATH RATTLERS.** VMF-323 was commissioned on August 1, 1943, flying the F4U Corsair and ended service in World War II with an outstanding combat record. In July 1950, 323 returned to combat in the Korean War as one of the earliest squadrons to arrive. Upon returning to MCAS El Toro in 1953, the unit received its first jets, the F9F Panther. In September 1956, it received the FJ-4 Fury and was redesignated VMF-323. (Courtesy George Dietsch.)

**VMFA-323 DEATH RATTLERS.** The last of the naval Furies was the FJ-4. Some people argue that the FJ-4 was the best version of the entire F-86 Sabre/FJ Fury series. The FJ-4 at first glance appears to be a modified F-86 Sabre that had first flown back in 1947. However, when one looks closer, it has many differences and only the family ancestry is apparent. The Fury's origins are rooted in a Navy requirement for a maximum speed of Mach 0.95 and an altitude of 49,000 feet, requirements not met before using an after-burning engine. (Courtesy FLAM.)

**VMFA-225 VIKINGS.** Commissioned at MCAS Mojave, California, on January 1, 1943, as VMF-225 the squadron flew the F4U-1 Corsair. In the fall of that year, 225 was deployed to Hawaii and to the New Hebrides Islands flying air defense combat missions. In May of 1945, 225 returned to the United States where it was deactivated in 1946. In 1948, 225 was reactivated at Cherry Point, North Carolina, and spent the next four years deploying from the East Coast on carriers to the Mediterranean and Caribbean Seas. This VMF-225 F4U Corsair flew in the 1946 National Air Races. (Courtesy FLAM.)

**VMFA-225 VIKINGS.** In 1966, 225 received the A6-A Intruder and was redesignated VMA(AW)225 and adopted the Vikings logo. In 1969, 225 was deployed to Danang Air Base, Vietnam and provided close air support for allied forces in the I Corps Area and interdiction missions along the Ho Chi Minh Trail. In 1971, 225 returned to MCAS El Toro and, once again, was deactivated. In 1991, 225 was reactivated with the F/A-18D Hornet at MCAS El Toro and relocated to MCAS Miramar in 1995. (Courtesy George Dietsch.)

**VMFAT-101 Sharpshooters.** Marine Fighter Attack Training Squadron 101 (VMFAT-101), the Sharpshooters, were commissioned at MCAS El Toro on January 3, 1969. The squadron trained naval aviators and naval flight officers in the employment of the McDonnell Douglas F-4 Phantom II. On September 29, 1987, VMFAT-101 returned from Yuma to MCAS El Toro to prepare for duty as the third F/A-18 Fleet Replacement Squadron (FRS). (Courtesy George Dietsch.)

**VMFAT-101 Sharpshooters.** This F/A-18 Hornet is painted in "aggressor" markings and is used to train pilots in air-to-air combat skills and tactics. Although Miramar's famous Top Gun school has relocated to Fallen, Nevada, the VMFAT-101 Sharpshooters maintain the tradition and are training the finest combat pilots, in the best equipment, in the history of the naval service. (Courtesy George Dietsch.)

**VMGR-352 RAIDERS.** Commissioned as Marine Utility Squadron 352 (VMJ-352) at MCAS Cherry Point on April 1, 1943, to its current designation as VMGR-352 based at MCAS Miramar, the Raiders have experienced a varied and colorful background. The squadron initially flew the Douglas R4D Skytrain aircraft, which it retained until its designation as Marine Transport Squadron 352 (VMR-352) in June 1944. In 1949, the squadron relocated to MCAS El Toro and supported the war in Korea. (Courtesy FLAM.).

**VMGR-352 RAIDERS.** In 1961, 352 became Marine Aerial Refueler Transport Squadron 352 (VMGR-352) with the arrival of the KC-130 Hercules. The squadron conducted its first TransPac (from California to Japan or Okinawa) operations in January 1962, moving VMF-451 and its squadron of 18 F8U's from MCAS El Toro to MCAS Iwakuni, Japan. The Raiders were called upon during the Cuban Missile Crisis in 1962 and the Dominican Republic in 1965. In June 1965, 352 began deploying in support of combat operations in the Republic of Vietnam and continued to do so until October 1972. (Courtesy FLAM.)

**MAG 13 Logo.** MAG-13, now located at MCAS Yuma, was initially activated March 1, 1942, at San Diego and participated in the Marshall Islands campaign during World War II. Deactivated at the close of the war, it was reactivated in March 1951. Since then, MAG-13 has deployed to Hawaii, Japan, and Vietnam, returning to El Toro in October 1970 and to Yuma on October 1, 1987. The MAG is comprised of Marine Aviation Logistics Squadron-13 and Marine Attack Squadrons 211, 214, 311, and 513.

**MCAS Yuma Logo.** In 1928, a parcel of land seven miles east of Yuma was leased from the federal government to become a military installation. During World War II, the base served as one of the Army's busiest flying schools. In 1951, it became the Weapons Proficiency Center for Western Air Defense Command. In 1956, the Air Force took over and the base became Vincent Air Force Base and home of the 4750th Air Defense Wing. In 1959, the base was acquired by the Navy and became Marine Corps Auxiliary Air Station.

**VMA-211 AVENGERS.** VMA-211 began as Fighter Squadron 4M in 1937, flying the Grumman F-3F biplane fighter aircraft at Naval Air Station North Island. The squadron moved to Ewa, Hawaii, in January 1941 and was redesignated as VMF-211 while transitioning to Grumman F4F-3 Wildcats. In November 1941, VMF-211 flew 12 Wildcats aboard the USS Enterprise for movement to Wake Island, the scene of the Marine Corps's and 211's heroic defense of Wake Island. (Courtesy FLAM.).

**VMA-211 AVENGERS.** The first Marine airman to be awarded the Medal of Honor in World War II was VMF-211's Capt. Henry "Hammering Hank" Elrod for heroic actions defending Wake Island. On December 25, 1941, Wake Island was finally overrun by a numerically superior enemy. The squadron's rear echelon was subsequently transferred to Palmyra Atoll in the South Pacific and adopted the name Avengers in memory of those squadron members who were killed or captured on Wake Island. They flew F4U Corsairs for the remainder of the war. (Courtesy VMA 211.)

**VMA-311 HELL'S BELLES.** Initially commissioned on December 1, 1942, at Cherry Point, North Carolina, flying the SNJ Texan trainers, 311 received the new F4U-1 Corsair in April 1943 and entered the Pacific Theater and combat operations until the end of World War II. After the war, VMF-311 moved to Yokosuka, Japan, as part of the occupational forces. The nickname Hell's Belles was adopted by the squadron during World War II, but was seldom used. In April 1948, the unit received the first jet aircraft to be introduced to Marine aviation, the Shooting Star. (Courtesy FLAM.)

**VMA-311 TOMCATS.** With the outbreak of war in Korea, the squadron moved to Pusan, Korea, flying the F9F Panther, providing close air support for 8th Army units near the Chosin Reservoir. It was early in 1957 that VMF-311 began to be referred to as the Tomcats. This period also brought the new Grumman F9F-8 Cougar, upgrading the squadron's capabilities. On June 1, 1957, the unit was redesignated Marine Attack Squadron-311, and in the summer of 1958 VMA-311 began receiving the Douglas A4D2 Skyhawks, later redesignated the A-4B. (Courtesy VMA-311.)

**VMA-214 BLACKSHEEP.** VMA-214 was originally commissioned on July 1, 1942, at Ewa, Hawaii. Initially called the Swashbucklers, they were disbanded following their first combat tour and the squadron designation was given to a Marine command on Espiritu Santo. In August 1943, a group of 27 young men under the leadership of Maj. "Pappy" Boyington joined together to form the original Blacksheep of VMF-214. The call sign was chosen by the squadron to commemorate the unusual way in which the squadron had been formed. (Courtesy FLAM.)

**VMA-214 BLACKSHEEP.** The pilots of 214 chose to carry into battle the black shield of illegitimacy, the "bar sinister," and a black sheep superimposed, surrounded by a circle of 12 stars and crowned with the image of their aircraft, the F4U-1 Corsair. The Blacksheep fought their way to fame in just 84 days. They met the Japanese and recorded a record 203 planes destroyed or damaged, produced 8 aces with 97 confirmed air-to-air kills, sunk several troop transports and supply ships, and destroyed many installations. (Courtesy FLAM.)

**VMA-513 NIGHTMARES.** This squadron was commissioned on February 15, 1944, at MCAF Oak Grove, North Carolina, flying the F6F Hellcat. On June 15, 1945, VMF(CVS)-513 departed San Diego for combat operations in the Pacific. After World War II, 513 operated from MCAS El Toro, transitioning to the F4U-5N, and was redesignated VMF(N)-513 Night Fighters. In 1952, VMF(N)-513 received the F-3D Skynight, the squadron's first jet aircraft, and made aviation history with the first radar kill on an enemy jet aircraft at night during the Korean War. (Courtesy FLAM.)

**VMA-513 NIGHTMARES.** VMA-513 has long been known for its aviation firsts, which include the first kill of a supersonic drone with a sidewinder missile in 1964, the first USMC squadron to transition to the AV-8A Harrier in 1970, the only squadron in the world to simultaneously employ all three variants of the AV-8B in 2001, and the first squadron to utilize the Lightening II Targeting Pod in combat in 2002. Now operating both the Night Attack and Radar variants of the Harrier, the Nightmares continue to develop STOVL concepts. (Courtesy FLAM.)

**MACG 38 Headquarters.** This squadron was commissioned September 1, 1967, at El Toro as Marine Air Control Group 38 and assigned to the Third Marine Aircraft Wing. MACG-38 participated in Operations Desert Shield and Desert Storm, Southwest Asia (August 1990–April 1991) and elements participated in Operation Restore Hope, Somalia (December 1992–March 1993) and Operation Safe Departure, Eritrea (June 1998). The group relocated in October 1998 to MCAS Miramar, subsequently participating in Operation Enduring Freedom.

**Marine Wing Support Group 37 Logo.** MWSG-37 was commissioned on July 1, 1953, in Miami, Florida, as Marine Wing Service Group 37. It was relocated to El Toro, California, in 1955 and redesignated as MWSG 37. The mission is to provide combat service support to the 3d Marine Aircraft Wing that includes, but is not limited to, motor transport, engineers, launch and recovery, and expeditionary airfield support. In 1985, 37 assumed responsibility for all air-wing aviation ground support. MWSG-37 has four MWSS squadrons: 371, 372, 373, and 374.

# *Six*

# MARINE CORPS AIR STATION MIRAMAR

MCAS Miramar has a long history as a Navy/Marine Corps facility supporting Marines and Sailors training to become proficient in aviation combat. The 3d Marine Aircraft Wing is the aviation combat element stationed at Miramar while the facilities, schools, simulators, and fixed assets are maintained by a separate command under the station commanding general. Maintaining the entire base and providing facilities for its entire compliment of military and civilian personnel is an enormous undertaking providing, in recent years, an economic impact on San Diego of nearly $600 million annually.

Among the most significant contributors to Miramar's operational success is the airfield operations department. "Base Ops," which includes a myriad of departments ranging from the control tower, weather, radar, the VAL line, crash crew, and the fuel farms, is responsible for keeping the airfield in operational order. Another significant contributor in making Miramar a functional training base is the base training department. The training department directly or indirectly controls and/or coordinates training for flight simulators, water survival, the rifle and pistol-range, gas masks, and physical and martial arts to name a few. The base public works department is responsible for maintaining existing structures, roads, and facilities, and for new construction that exceeded $363 million in 1999 while the Marines were upgrading the entire base to almost $38 million in 2003.

The Miramar Marines have created a first-class military installation as modern as any in the world and are supporting the nation's defense and war on terrorism in a first-class manner.

**MCAS Miramar Logo.** The MCAS logo was created when the Marines returned to Miramar in 1997. The eagle, globe and anchor, with a Corsair in the center of a red triangle, are taken from the original depot logo dating to World War II. The red diamond in the center background is taken from Marine air wing logos representing Marine aviation, while the lightning bolts signify Marine air power. Jets and helicopters are represented at MCAS Miramar. San Diego's coastline is depicted at the bottom of the logo, giving a geographical reference for the base.

**Headquarters.** The MCAS headquarters building is home to the commanding general of Marine Corps Air Bases Western Area, which includes MCAS Yuma, MCAS Camp Pendleton, and MCAS Miramar. The command's mission is to provide support of assigned aeronautical shore activities to aviation units of the West Coast Fleet Marine Forces. The station maintains all the fixed assets, buildings, roads, and supports all the Marines stationed at Miramar.

**C-12 HURON BY CONTROL TOWER.** The C-12 Huron is a twin-engine aircraft with the mission of carrying passengers and cargo between military installations. Powered by two PT-6A-42 turboprop engines, the C-12F can deliver a total payload of up to 4,215 pounds. The cabin can readily accommodate cargo, passengers, or both. It is also equipped to accept litter patients in medical evacuation missions. The cost for a C-12 is around $2 million and cruising speed is 294 knots with a range of 1,974 nautical miles. This C-12 is parked by Miramar's control tower. (Courtesy George Dietsch.)

**AIRCRAFT RESCUE/FIRE FIGHTING/RECOVERY (AARF) P-19s.** The P-19 fire-fighting vehicle used by the Marine Corps is capable of operations in nuclear, biological, and chemical threat conditions, in extreme weather, and over varying terrain. Designed to operate at expeditionary airfields in remote areas, the P19 provides fire-fighting capabilities and performs aircrew rescue operations. These P-19s are lined up in front of Miramar's base operations building. (Courtesy George Dietsch.)

**AARF FIGHTING FIRES.** The AARF personnel regularly practice their craft. Extinguishing fires on aircraft, sometimes laden with ordnance, is one of the most demanding and dangerous jobs in the Marine Corps.

**REDEDICATED BOB HOPE THEATER.** This is the original theater built at Miramar back in the 1940s. It has recently been renovated and dedicated in honor of Bob Hope, the famous comedian and star of countless USO shows.

**CH53E Super Stallions Staged for Deployment.** These Super Stallions are staged on the MCAS Miramar flight line for loading and deployment. The rotor blades and main transmission are removed and staged behind each helicopter in order for the Super Stallion to be loaded into an Air Force C-5 Galaxy transport aircraft. Helicopter mechanics have become so skilled at this procedure that they can have the Super Stallions off-loaded and ready for test flight within hours after landing at their destination. (Courtesy George Dietsch.)

**CH53E Super Stallions on Board C-5 Galaxy.** With inches to spare, this CH53E Super Stallion is loaded onboard a C-5 Galaxy. The C-5 Galaxy can transport two CH53E Super Stallions with its entire compliment of blades, parts, and crew to just about anywhere in the world. (Courtesy George Dietsch.)

**UH-1N Search and Rescue Helicopter.** This UH-1N helicopter is from MCAS Yuma and is parked by Miramar's control tower. (Courtesy George Dietsch.)

**Marines Deploying to the Middle East.** MCAS Miramar is the Marine Corps's primary West Coast "point of departure" for Marines heading overseas. A variety of carriers can be seen departing Miramar, ranging from U.S. Air Force C-5 and C-17 transports to commercial airliners. Miramar is a full-service airfield with runways and support facilities to accommodate the mission. (Courtesy George Dietsch.)

**STATION TRAINING DEPARTMENT.** The station-training department is one of the most important departments on the air station. It is in charge of operating everything from several different state-of-the-art aircraft flight simulators, to the base swimming pool, ranges, and gas mask and martial arts training.

**GAS-MASK TRAINING.** Among every Marine's least favorite phases is "gas mask training." Donning, clearing, and breathing through a gas mask in 11 seconds is a standard test in the Marine Corps. To make sure each individual Marine's gas mask fits properly, they walk them through the gas chamber and detonate a tear-gas grenade. Once assured the mask fits properly, each Marine is ordered to remove the mask and recite his name, rank, and serial number. Then the gunny says, "Pain is good for your character." (Courtesy USN.)

**SIMULATOR TRAINING ON FIGHTERS.** Modern simulators are becoming more sophisticated each year, providing pilots with the ability to practice emergency procedures and aircraft skills that otherwise would have to be done in an aircraft. Simulators reduce overall costs of training and enhance pilot skills dramatically before the pilot ever "straps on" his aircraft. (Courtesy USN.)

**SIMULATOR TRAINING ON MULTI-ENGINE AIRCRAFT.** Try to imagine learning what every gauge, switch, and knob in this multi-engine aircraft does before going on your first flight. This plane provides an incredible training experience that reduces pilot errors in flight. (Courtesy USN.)

**AVIATION SURVIVAL TRAINING CENTER.**
The Navy and the Marine Corps obviously spend a significant amount of their time flying over water, and occasionally they end up in the water. Very often that experience is fatal. Naval aviators must be trained in the many aspects of water and land survival.

**DILBERT DUNKER, WATER SURVIVAL TRAINING.** This device is among the most favorite helicopter-training aids. Helicopter aircrews climb into the large, red cabin at the top of the rails and strap themselves in tight. The cabin slides down the rails into the water and then rolls upside down. Once upside down the passengers are permitted to escape from their craft, simulating crashing into the water. After several successful escapes, students are required to perform a successful escape blindfolded. (Courtesy USN.)

**MODERN DUNKER.** The older Dunkers sat two people side-by-side, and then larger Dunkers sat 8 to 10 people. Trying to evacuate from an inverted, 10-passenger Dunker blindfolded is an experience most could do without. There is little danger of drowning, because divers are under the water to guarantee safety. The biggest danger is catching a foot in the face from the person ahead of you. (Courtesy USN.)

**MODERN BARRACKS.** Upon their return to Miramar in the 1990s, the Marine Corps spent substantial sums of money rehabilitating the base. New roads, buildings, and facilities were built to make Miramar a 21st-century site for a modern Marine Corps. New barracks were constructed to accommodate the many squadrons relocating to Miramar.

**OLD BUILDINGS.** Despite the enormous rehabilitation effort undertaken when the Marines relocated to Miramar, many old buildings can be found all over the air station. This building dates to Miramar's earliest days and is currently used as a warehouse.

**OLD BUILDINGS.** Modern vehicles, parked in front of this 1940s building, provide an unusual contrast. However, the legal assistance office functions just as efficiently despite the building's age.

**COLOR GUARD BY UC-35.** The UC-35 is a modified version of the Cessna Citation corporate passenger jet. It is used by the Marines for passenger and cargo transportation, and for training purposes. The station color guard passes by this UC-35 during a change of command ceremony for the base commanding general. (Courtesy George Dietsch.)

**PRESIDENTIAL VISIT.** One of the high points of serving at MCAS Miramar occurred when Pres. George W. Bush visited the base in Air Force One. He gave a speech on the flight line and visited with individual Marines, genuinely thanking everyone for their service, dedication, and contributions to the defense of liberty and democracy. (Courtesy USMC.)

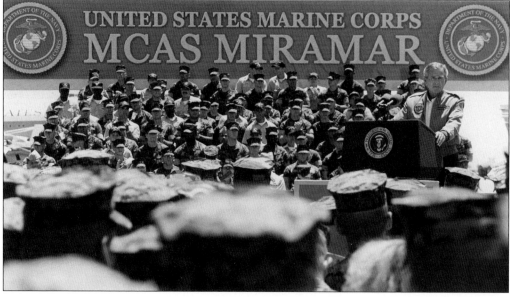

# Seven

# MARINE AIRCRAFT GROUP 46, 4TH MARINE AIRCRAFT WING

Marine Aircraft Group 46 (MAG46) is the 4th Marine Aircraft Wing's premier West Coast reserve aviation group. The Marine Corps has three active duty air wings: the 1st, 2nd, and 3rd, and one reserve air wing, the 4thMAW. MAG-46 is one of six MAGs in the 4thMAW and is located at MCAS Miramar. MAG-46 has two detachments: Detachment A, located at Camp Pendleton and consisting of HMLA-775, and Detachment B, located at Edwards Air Force Base and consisting of HMH-769 and HMM-764. VMFA-134 is located at MCAS Miramar and VMFT-401 is located at Yuma. West Coast Marine reserve air units represent a cross-section of an active-duty air wing. Reserve units in MAG-46 fly Hornets, Super Stallions, Sea Knights, Cobras, and Hueys, while VMFT-401 flies the F5E Tiger II.

Marine Air Reserve Training Command (MARTC) was established to preserve the skills learned during World War II. That foresight paid off in 1950 when the Korean War broke out and the reserves provided a significant force of trained "citizen" warriors. With a force of 6,035 Marines, MARTC was prepared for mobilization and fielded three fighter squadrons in Korea less than two weeks after mobilization. The value of reservist, "citizen warriors" dates to the Revolutionary War and is recognized as a vital element of our national defense. The Marine Corps Reserve, arguably the best-trained and most professional military reserve component in any of the armed forces, and particularly MAG-46, is a shining example of that heritage.

**MAG-46 Logo.** MAG-46 is the 4th Marine Aircraft Wing's West Coast aircraft group and consists of five reserve flying squadrons. The MAG-46 headquarters coordinates logistics, administration, and training for its squadrons, as well as units deploying overseas in support of Operation Iraqi Freedom. The distinguished heritage of the reserves continues as many reserve units serve in Iraq and Afghanistan, fighting the war on terror.

**VMFT-401 Snipers, F-5 Tiger II.** VMFT-401 is a reserve squadron, and part of MAG-46, located at MCAS Yuma. Duty in 401 is one of the best-kept secrets in any branch of the service. Currently flying the Northrop F-5 Tiger fighter in the role of an aggressor squadron, the pilots of 401 enjoy the best flying—most of the time. VMFT-401 has also flown the F-21 Israeli KFIR. (Courtesy George Dietsch.)

**HMH-769 ROADHOGS.** The Roadhogs are undoubtedly the 4th Marine Aircraft Wing's most combat-tested and proficient heavy-lift squadron. It was deployed to the Middle East for the Desert Storm War and again to Afghanistan in 2004 to support the war on terrorism. The squadron maintains the highest aircraft readiness, training levels, and dedication, often in the face of overwhelming obstacles and not always with the best support. The Roadhogs have been the embodiment of the citizen warrior serving a nation. (Courtesy George Dietsch.)

**HMLA-775 COYOTES.** HMA-775 is a reserve squadron and was established on January 7, 1989, at MCAS Camp Pendleton. Flight operations commenced with 12 AH-1J (1968 AH-1J's) Sea Cobras. On December 1, 1990, HMA 775 was activated in support of Operation Desert Shield. In June 1994, five UH-1N helicopters were accepted and the squadron was redesignated Marine Light Attack Helicopter Squadron 775 (HMLA-775), becoming the first HMLA in the Fourth Marine Aircraft Wing (4th MAW). (Courtesy George Dietsch.)

**VMFA-134.** This squadron was activated May 1, 1943, at Santa Barbara, California, as Marine Scout Bombing Squadron 134 and was assigned to Marine Base Defense Aircraft Group 42, Marine Fleet Air, West Coast. The squadron was redesignated June 1, 1943, as Marine Torpedo Bombing Squadron 134 and was deployed during October–November 1943 to the South Pacific to support combat operations. Deactivated at the end of World War II, the squadron stood up again on April 15, 1958, as a reserve squadron at Los Alamitos, California. (Courtesy George Dietsch.)

**HMM-764 MOONLIGHTERS.** The HMM-764 Moonlighters have a long history and proud tradition of able and dedicated reserve Marines contributing to the defense of the nation. Flying the CH-46 Sea Knight, the Moonlighters also have a long history of moving—from Los Alamitos to MCAS Tustin, to MCAS El Toro and eventually MCAS Miramar. Flying one of the oldest helicopters in any military inventory, the Moonlighters make up in dedication what they lose in technology. (Courtesy FLAM.)

# *Eight*

# FLYING LEATHERNECK AVIATION MUSEUM

The Flying Leatherneck Aviation Museum (FLAM) is a MCAS Miramar command museum under the Commanding General Marine Corps Bases Western Area in conjunction with the Marine Corps History and Museum Division at Quantico. The FLAM is the Marine Corps' only "aviation" museum, although the Corps' National Museum at Quantico also offers aviation displays. The FLAM has 43 total aircraft with approximately 30 on display outdoors at any one time, as well as approximately 3,000 square feet of indoor gallery display space with a very nice collection of aviation art, models, memorabilia, artifacts, and uniforms. Displays of women marines, prisoners-of-war, and early Marine aviation are among visitor favorites. The FLAM boasts a first-class restoration facility in its 27,000-square-foot warehouse where aircraft are taken apart and restored from the inside out to preserve these historic treasures for generations to come. New aircraft are always being pursued by museum staff and several additions are currently scheduled to join the FLAM's outstanding collection. The FLAM's displays are supported by dozens of incredible volunteers who greet visitors, provide directions and educational tours, and serve as security. The FLAM's mission is to collect, preserve, display, and memorialize the achievements, success, contributions, and failures of Marine aviation. It isn't to glorify war, but to educate current Marines about the heritage they have inherited and to enlighten the public about Marine Corps contributions to national security and world peace. The aircraft in this chapter are all museum-display aircraft.

**FLAM Logo.** The Flying Leatherneck Aviation Museum logo combines the Marine Corps's first aviation logo used in World War I on a gold shield. The Flying Leatherneck Aviation Museum is the Marine Corps's first and only aviation museum, providing a distant connection. Although the mission of Marine aviation is to support Marines on the ground, it has its own unique history, heroes, and tales to tell.

**F4U-5N Corsair, "Whistling Death."** The F4U Corsair was in production longer than any of the American-built World War II fighters initially flying on May 29, 1940, and continued in production until December 1952. The Marine Corps first deployed the Corsair during World War II in February 1943 with VMF-124 at Bougainville, where famous Aces like Pappy Boyington, Ken Walsh, Joe Foss, and others terrorized the Japanese, and where the Japanese named the Corsair "Whistling Death" because of the sound the aircraft made in a steep dive. This aircraft has VMF(N)-513 markings. (Courtesy George Dietsch.)

**SNJ Texan.** North American Aircraft Manufacturers built nearly 16,000 Texan trainers during World War II for the U.S. Armed Forces and their allies. The Navy and Marine Corps operated nearly 5,000 Texans, and they have been used in over 30 different countries. This Texan sits behind the museum's temporary, 4,200-square-foot buildings that are filled with displays, memorabilia, photographs, artifacts, and a gift shop. (Courtesy George Dietsch.)

**Helicopter Displays.** The museum grounds offer a rolling, landscaped area where visitors can leisurely walk the grounds and closely view the static aircraft displays. The helicopter side of the museum includes the H-19 Chickasaw, the H-34 Sea Horse, the Iraqi Bell 214, the CH-53A Sea Stallion, the AH-1J Cobra, the HUP Retriever, and the HOK Huskie. The Bell HTL-4 has just been restored, while the UH-1 is in storage awaiting refurbishment. The many grassy areas around the aircraft are used frequently for parties and ceremonies. (Courtesy George Dietsch.)

**JET DISPLAYS.** On the other side of the museum, the FLAM's jets are on display. The museum has a good variety of jet aircraft ranging, from the TO-1 Shooting Star, which was the first mass-produced jet in the late 1940s, to modern-day jets including an F/A-18A Hornet. Names like Banshee and Fury stir the blood of those who served in Korean War–era aviation, while Phantom, Skyhawk, and Intruder relate to the Vietnam War era. An F8E Crusader is the museum's most recent restoration success. (Courtesy George Dietsch.)

**B-25 MITCHELL.** The B-25 Mitchell may be most famous for participating in Doolittle's Raid on Tokyo early in World War II. The Marine Corps had seven B-25 squadrons in combat during World War II that flew the first night raids at Rabaul, Kavieng, and Bougainville against Japanese positions. The B-25 provided an ideal weapons platform with forward-firing, .50-caliber machine guns in addition to overhead and belly-gun turrets. Several B-25s (G/H models) were armed with a 75-mm, forward-firing cannon. (Courtesy George Dietsch.)

**WILDCAT.** Grumman Aircraft Company designed and built the Wildcat prior to World War II. During the early years of the war, Grumman switched production to other aircraft, and General Motors began producing the Wildcat. Eleven Marine Wildcat squadrons were credited with shooting down 562 enemy aircraft during the war. This plane crashed into Lake Michigan while training during the war, and sat at the bottom of the lake for 45 years until the Navy's Pensacola, Florida, museum rescued and restored it. (Courtesy George Dietsch.)

**F9F PANTHER.** The Panther first flew in November 1947 while the first production model launched in February 1949. It was the Navy/Marine Corps's first jet to see combat. VMF-311 was the first Marine squadron to fly the Panther and the first to enter the Korean War combat zone. The Panther was no match for the swept-wing MiG-15, deployed by the North Koreans, Russians, and Chinese during the Korean War, and was soon replaced by the Fury.

**FJ3 FURY**. The Fury was initially designed as a straight-winged fighter and first flew in November 1946. However, with the success of the Russian MiG-15 fighter against the straight-winged Panther during aerial combat, the Fury was modified. Later models of the Fury were navalized versions of the USAF F-86 Sabre Jet. The Fury's armament consisted of four 20-mm cannons and up to six missiles. The Fury was also capable of carrying nuclear weapons.

**F8E CRUSADER**. In 1952, the Navy announced a requirement for a MACH-1 fighter. The first Crusader flew in March 1955 and flew in excess of the speed of sound on its first flight. The most unique feature on the Crusader is the variable-incidence wing that raised and lowered seven degrees, acting as a giant flap permitting slower speeds during takeoff and landing. The Crusader was also the first carrier-based aircraft that could fly over 1,000 miles per hour. In the early 1960s, a new designation system was adopted and this Crusader became an F8E Crusader. (Courtesy George Dietsch.)

**H-34 Sea Horse.** The H-34 entered Marine Corps units in 1957 and was best known in the Marine Corps for its service during Operation "Shu-Fly" in Vietnam during the early 1960s. Although vastly superior to its predecessors, the H-34 was soon replaced by the CH-46A and CH-53A. This H-34, shown in restoration, was previously painted the wrong color with dissimilar paints that were causing a chemical reaction and accelerating corrosion. The restorers had to strip the aircraft to bare metal before painting.

**CH-53A Sea Stallion.** The CH-53A entered service in 1966, serving as a heavy lift, cargo, and troop transport helicopter designed to enhance the capability of commanders in combat theaters to insert/extract troops and/or artillery where needed. The CH-53A could carry 35 fully armed combat troops. Secondary missions included cargo drops, para-operations, medical evacuations, search and rescue, and downed-pilot rescues. The CH-53's cruising airspeed was 170 knots (203 miles per hour) and its gross maximum weight was 42,000 pounds. (Courtesy George Dietsch.)

**VOLUNTEERS.** Upon relocation to MCAS Miramar from MCAS El Toro in 1998, Steve Smith (left) and Dave Koning (right) represented two of the museum's three employees and were individually responsible for performing much of the work necessary to raise a museum from ground zero. Generally unheralded museum employees often work from a "labor of love," performing small miracles. Andrew O'Hara (center) is one of several very dedicated restoration volunteers who, in addition to 60 to 70 docents, keep the museum going.

**WANTED: A FEW GOOD RESTORATION VOLUNTEERS.** Mike Sherlock, the museum's premier restoration volunteer, took this tug from the scrap heap and restored it to like-new condition. Mike never worked in aviation, but he took a disassembled Bell HTL-4 helicopter and put it back together again after fully restoring, fabricating, and/or manufacturing each part. The aviation museum business can only survive through the efforts of volunteers like Mike who give much of their time and skill to preserve history.